Praise for
Overcoming Perfectionism

"As I discuss in my new book *Recover to Live: Kick Any Habit, Manage Any Addiction*, you can't lead a productive and fulfilling life if [illegible] balance [illegible]. Perfectionism can be just as damaging as [illegible] other compulsive behaviors. Ann Smith is [illegible] helping people to break lifelong patterns and find balance in their lives. I would highly recommend this book."

—Christopher Kennedy Lawford

"As a former Miss USA, I've devoted a lot of time to trying to be the perfect woman. In fact, I spent so much time trying to be the Tara that everyone else wanted me to be that I wasn't in touch with my own needs. [illegible] me to develop and live in sync with my own values and authentic self. She has empowered me to love the woman I am today. I would recommend this book to anyone seeking self-acceptance."

—Tara Conner, Miss USA 2006, [illegible] Advocate/Consultant, Caron Treatment Centers

"The drive for perfection is a painful dynamic that destroys relationships and leads to a life of despair, emptiness, and exhaustion. Ann Smith has taken her seminal work on perfectionism and created an inspirational and practical guide! I'd recommend this book for anyone who is plagued by patterns of perfectionistic thinking or behavior!"

—**Rokelle Lerner**, Author of *The Object of my Affection Is in My Reflection: Coping with Narcissists*; Clinical Director Cottonwood Inner Path Workshops

"I highly recommend Ann Smith's second edition of her highly successful book, *Overcoming Perfectionism*. She has taken her work to another level, one that will benefit all who are making the journey beyond their painful childhoods. Her work is very personal, but her willingness to share her knowledge and emotions will touch many readers. Her style of writing makes you feel that this book is just for you and so it is."

—**Robert J. Ackerman, PhD,** Author, *Perfect Daughters: Adult Daughters of Alcoholics*, Professor and Program Director of the Human Services Degree Program at the University of South Carolina at Beaufort.

REVISED & UPDATED

OVERCOMING PERFECTIONISM

Finding the Key to Balance & Self-Acceptance

Ann W. Smith, MS

Health Communications, Inc.
Deerfield Beach, Florida
www.hcibooks.com

Library of Congress Cataloging-in-Publication Data

Smith, Ann W., 1950-
Overcoming perfectionism : finding the key to balance and self-acceptance / by Ann W. Smith, MS.
pages cm
Includes bibliographical references.
ISBN-13: 978-0-7573-1720-0 (pbk.)
ISBN-10: 0-7573-1720-0 (pbk.)
ISBN-13: 978-0-7573-1721-7 (e-book)
ISBN-10: 0-7573-1721-9 (e-book)
1. Perfectionism (Personality trait) 2. Codependency. 3. Compulsive behavior—Treatment. I. Title.
RC569.5.P45S65 2013
616.85'2—dc23

2013001568

Publisher: Health Communications, Inc.
3201 S.W. 15th Street
Deerfield Beach, FL 33442-8190

Cover design by Lawna Patterson Oldfield
Interior design and formatting by Dawn Von Strolley Grove

To

Marilyn Hawn,

my friend,

confidante, role model,

and lifelong inspiration

Contents

Introduction

Writing a second edition of *Overcoming Perfectionism* has been an enjoyable and validating exercise for me. I do love to write, but I find it difficult to create the space and time to do it as much as I would like. This project has allowed me to go back to my own beginnings—as a therapist, a mom, an aunt, a wife, a sister, a daughter, a teacher, a director, and a friend—and reflect on what I have learned and how I have grown. At the same time, I can see that my essence has not really changed all that much.

When I wrote the original *Overcoming Perfectionism*, I was a single mom with two children, ages seven and seventeen. I had just left my full-time job, moved sixty miles away, and built an irrationally large, six-bedroom house for my seven-year-old daughter, Lindsay, and myself. My son, Jeff, was going off to college, and I started my own business. I met the man who became my husband and married him soon after, expanding my little family with three more boys. We were a very nontraditional family with what seemed like a revolving door on our house. "Build it and they will come" was a frequent comment made by friends and extended family that proved to be very true.

During our first ten years in the big house, we were frustrated with the chronic problem of two leaking chimneys that made a mess of our two attic bedrooms. The builder brought in experts and tried everything the team could think of to fix the chimneys. They would be okay for a while, but then the leaking would start again. At the ten-year point, we thought we had it permanently repaired.

My husband helped me to expand my business during those years, and we were a good team. Through his career as a training director, he just happened to have the skills I lacked. This helped a great deal with my start-up private practice and five-and-a-half-day workshops.

As we approached an empty nest, breathing a sigh of relief that our five children were almost adults, we considered selling the big house and downsizing. After months of preparing for the move and having many showings, we were forced to take the house off the market because the leaks in the chimneys returned, and the house was just too big for most people.

We were also exhausted from the challenges of a blended family and raising so many teenagers, so we decided to enjoy our space while we figured out what was next for us. After three years of relative quiet, we decided to prepare the house for sale once again. Within what seemed like just a few days after that decision, the water heater gave out and a torrential rain caused the chimneys to leak once more, damaging the ceilings and leaving us no choice but to postpone the sale. With this setback, we were again in pause mode, when the unthinkable happened.

My husband's sister and her husband, who lived in a nearby town, were tragically killed, leaving three young children and two adult sons without parents. It was traumatic for everyone concerned and had a ripple effect throughout all of our lives. Our "pause" was then transformed, and all of our lives were sent in an entirely new direction.

In a few months, my husband and I were active parents once again, to three children ages twelve, fifteen, and sixteen. All available space in our big house was full once again. Then, much to our amazement, one week before the children arrived at our doorstep, a contractor we had not heard from in many months contacted us, saying that he had found a permanent solution to our leaking chimneys after fourteen years of trial and error. We were so grateful to have what we later called our "house that God built." And although it was a tough adjustment for all of us, the children got exactly what they needed. They were secure in their own dry bedrooms, and more important, they were safe and loved by a family that shared and understood the trauma they had experienced. We are thankful that we have not had a single leak in seven years.

Today, the youngest of my sister-in-law's three children is in his first year of college, and her oldest daughter was married last month. My husband and I are alone again, preparing the house for sale, we hope for next year. Our six grandchildren are very fond of this house, and I know that they would want us to keep it forever. I have no solid plan, one way or the other. I have learned that if I just keep walking in the direction that feels best, things have a way of working out.

I would love to say that I handled everything with grace and patience, but that would not be true. It was very hard. Overall, I feel good about myself and believe that my marriage is the cornerstone of this story. There were many other difficult challenges that I don't dwell on or worry about today. I have learned how to love unconditionally, how to accept what is, and how to show up when called upon. Yet there is no end to the story—so much for being perfect.

When I wrote the first edition, I was doing the best I could with my life. I still am, but I no longer have an agenda of being great or proving that I am strong. That is the moral of this book: It is enough to just be you and put one foot in front of the other while doing the next best thing.

THE SECOND EDITION

There are a few significant changes in this edition, based on the evolution of the addiction and mental health fields. You will notice that the word *codependency* is no longer prominent in this book. We have reached a new level of understanding that I believe is more useful and applies to a much larger group of people who are stuck in dysfunctional relationship patterns and emotional pain. I have limited the use of other labels in this edition as well. For instance, family roles are not labeled as hero, scapegoat, and so forth, and the more inclusive term *painful family* is used in place of *alcoholic family.*

Based on experience with a wide range of clients, clinical professionals no longer consider the alcoholic family to be unique in its effect on individuals. In studying and working with families affected by addiction, we have learned a great deal, and as a result we have been able to help thousands of people open up about the challenges they experienced in childhood.

The second chapter explains the human experience in a broader sense than we had understood when the first book was written. It focuses on patterns developed in childhood as a result of insecure attachment when families are in pain or chronic stress. It is important to understand that this pattern is a normal human response, not a dysfunctional choice.

When an awareness of the negative effects of growing up in an alcoholic or chemically dependent family first gained attention during the late 1980s and the 1990s, droves of adult children of alcoholics came to conferences, read self-help books, and sought help at places like Breakthrough at Caron, then called Caron's Adult Children of Alcoholics program. Throughout my first eight years with the program, more than 14,000 people attended the five-and-a-half-day residential program. Since then, the total has been estimated at well over 35,000 and is growing. Many of these people's stories are in this book.

There is an increased emphasis in this edition on the covert perfectionist. The first chapter examines the similarities and differences between covert and overt perfectionism. It opens the door to a large group of people whose perfectionism exists more as a pattern of thinking than as obvious visible traits, but for the covert perfectionist this reality is equally troublesome. The approach in this book is designed to benefit both overt and covert perfectionists by increasing self-awareness and self-esteem through a process of letting go and learning self-acceptance.

My overall goal in writing this book is to improve your quality of life by showing you how to bring in more of what really matters to you and let go of what gets in the way of your peace of mind. I urge you to use it as a workbook. Take notes, write in the margins, and make it your own. The exercises were designed to show perfectionists how to live in the middle, to find their balance. I encourage you to find yours.

Chapter 1

Overt and Covert Perfectionism

Perfectionism is a fairly common phenomenon. It is natural for most of us to strive to overcome our human imperfections. No one enjoys making mistakes or exposing their flaws, nor do they appreciate the value of the experience of learning from one's mistakes. This tendency is exacerbated by our society, which feeds the belief that we can and should improve on any flaw—whether real or imagined—in our homes, our health, our parenting, our finances, and our relationships. The "experts" insist that there is always a better way.

We are told by the media, the workplace, the school system, and even by our families that we must always do our best. Messages such as "Anything worth doing is worth doing well" have reinforced the notion that if we can't do something extremely well, why bother doing it at all? "If you can do it better, you should!" Advances in technology have allowed us to do just that. We can search the Internet to find the perfect solution to any problem in minutes, whether it's breast-feeding, child rearing, money management, or a health problem.

Overall, there is nothing terribly wrong with trying to be the best we can be. Excellence, as a choice, can be very rewarding. There are a number of professions and tasks that require near perfection, because not meeting such high standards could ultimately be the deciding factor between life and death. Nik Wallenda's high-wire walk over Niagara Falls certainly qualifies. It is a life-and-death matter, but one that is not without flaws or missteps. I'd expect the endodontist who did my root canal to have perfected his technique, otherwise I will need another procedure in the future. The pilots who take off and land our planes need to be excellent, but we all know they aren't perfect. The same goes for air traffic controllers. We count on them, but we know they will make mistakes. While surgeons do their absolute best, they cannot be perfect. They can never control all the variables, and most important, they are human.

Professions or tasks that require excellence are among the most stressful and anxiety producing. They generally pay well, but some have higher suicide rates than others. This most likely results from the fact that those who seek out such professions are human, and human beings are not built to be perfect.

The desire to be superhuman becomes a problem when we begin to believe that perfection is actually possible and even necessary for self-esteem, success, peace of mind, and acceptance by others. We forget that we have a choice and that we will never reach the goal of perfection. It is at this point that the striving evolves into a compulsion.

Anyone with a minimal degree of honesty will be able to identify some form of troublesome compulsion in his or her life. We are inclined to repeat any behavior that feels good, even if the feeling is only temporary. Some of these compulsive patterns, such as eating disorders and chemical dependency, have a physiological component and may more accurately be termed *addictions*.

Addicts often have a physical craving for and dependence on a substance as well as a psychological need or compulsion to continue its use. In some addictions, individuals build up a physical tolerance to the substance and must use more and more to get the same effect. With process addictions, such as sex addiction, the arousal level begins to decrease over time to a degree that the frequency and intensity of the activity must increase to get the desired result. Addiction is believed to be caused by a combination of genetics, brain chemistry, metabolism, and environment. It is potentially fatal and has severe negative consequences. It is necessary for addicts to detoxify by abstaining before they can begin a psychological recovery.

Compulsion, in contrast, has been defined as "repeated action without choice."1 Compulsion may or may not have a physiological component, and it is often experienced as an unconscious urge, like an itch to scratch. As human beings, when we become uncomfortable—sometimes consciously, sometimes unconsciously—we turn to familiar behaviors or patterns to distract us from our discomfort.

1 I believe it is necessary to make a distinction between perfectionism and the psychiatric diagnosis of obsessive-compulsive disorder (OCD). OCD is a serious, debilitating form of mental illness believed to have a physiological basis. Its victims have what Dr. Judith L. Rapoport calls a "tic of the brain." Among its symptoms are compulsive hand washing, obsessions with numbers, or checking something over and over without cause. Rapoport also calls it the "doubting disease," since no amount of reason or reassurance will put to rest the belief that it is necessary to check the door, the gas, or the lights one more time.

Obsessive-compulsives aren't particularly perfectionist in most areas of their lives. Their illness often focuses on a specific behavior, such as how they go through a doorway or whether they are clean. The only way to stop the mental obsession is to perform the act again and again. Those seeking further information about OCD and its treatment may benefit from reading Judith L. Rapoport, *The Boy Who Couldn't Stop Washing: The Experience and Treatment of Obsessive Compulsive Disorder* (Markham, Ontario, Canada: New American Library, 1997).

It is highly unusual to find an individual who has only one compulsive behavior. We all seem to have our favorites, those on which we most frequently depend, and perhaps a few we reserve for special occasions, such as when we are happy or sad. Nail-biting, overeating, working, shopping, cleaning, smoking, exercising, sex, relationships, caretaking, worshiping, and gambling are only a few of the most common compulsions. Most of these are harmless, and many are enjoyable or at least soothing. Problems develop when we do them without conscious choice and they begin to have unwanted, negative consequences.

Joseph was in excellent physical condition as a result of daily jogging and workouts at the fitness center. Exercise was a very positive factor in his life until it began to replace other things that were once important to him—like family time, his marriage, and work advancement. Despite several injuries and surgeries, he persisted in his training. Eventually, Joseph no longer had any choice with his compulsive behavior. What was once a pleasure became a driving need. He was obsessed with his appearance, his running times, and his progress compared to other athletes. His training for marathons replaced family vacations. Without exercise, he was irritable, depressed, and anxious. Joseph was not aware of the negative effects until his marriage began to suffer, largely as a result of his lack of attention to the relationships with his wife and his children.

Joseph, like many people, denied he had a problem. But denial is, in fact, part of the problem, particularly when compulsive behavior is rewarded. In Joseph's case, he was admired by friends who often described him as a healthy, disciplined, and attractive man. While he was in good health, only his family was aware of the negative progression of his behavior.

Occasionally, a crisis or maybe an injury will cause the addict to stop abruptly and go into a period of psychological withdrawal. During this time, he or she may experience sudden rage, depression, sleeplessness, or a dramatic change in energy level. The feelings that the addict had been medicating with the compulsion now rise to the surface and seem to have no cause or explanation. A notable example is Olympian swimmer Michael Phelps's recent public divulgence of his bout with depression after winning eight gold medals at the 2008 Olympics. Though not technically considered an addiction, his training and commitment to his lifelong goal may have served as his only way of managing his emotions, and as a result his amazing success was followed by an emotional crash.

When Joseph reached the crisis point, he had three choices: resume his exercise, find something else to be compulsive about, or feel his discomfort and work through it. Most of us are so unconscious of this cycle that we instinctively find something else to ease the tension instead of exploring the deeper problem. Fortunately, Joseph chose to face his feelings. In therapy, he was able to work through the source of his compulsion and gradually let it go. In his case, perfectionism was part of the problem that led him into an excessive focus on his health and appearance. He would eventually have to address it in other areas of his life as well.

OVERT PERFECTIONISM

Perfectionism can be described as a compulsion, but for some, it is also part of their DNA, personality, and temperament. We all know someone who seems to be the stereotypical perfectionist: visibly organized, a little uptight about the details, and so forth. Throughout the book I will identify individuals with this type as overt perfectionists. Born with these tendencies, *overt perfectionists* are often more likely to enjoy order and structure from an early age. These tendencies will appear as a basic neutral trait and are not attributable to low self-esteem or insecurities.

I have observed happy, healthy toddlers lining up toys until they are in a straight line and rejoicing in the accomplishment. Behaviors like these are not good or bad. However, if a child has also developed insecurity as a reaction to negative or painful life experiences, these tendencies may intensify, becoming a pattern of compensation for the child not feeling loved or good enough. Depending on his or her personality and the degree of stress, the pattern can escalate into a lifetime pattern of perfectionism.

The overt, or visible, perfectionist always appears well put together: self-disciplined, neat, orderly, and prepared for anything. Judy, a former client, reluctantly described her perfectionism this way: "I keep everything in my purse anyone might ever need: scissors, Kleenex, comb, a sewing kit, aspirin, nail file, tweezers, and Band-Aids. I can't leave the house unless my hair is perfect and my children are clean and properly dressed the way I like, and I am ready for guests at all times—although I rarely have guests drop in." The spices in her kitchen were alphabetized, she never forgot a birthday, she always bought Christmas gifts well in advance, and she bought gifts for everyone she knew when she was on vacation. She was always on time and had the most organized desk in the real estate office where she worked part-time.

When Judy had a Christmas party, she put a Christmas tree in every room of her perfect house, and a little train ran around on a track hanging from the ceiling. Every spring she surrounded her yard with a perfect line of flowers, trimmed every bush, and repainted the front door. By the time she sought help, Judy was angry and depressed. Her husband was having an affair and wasn't sure whether he loved her anymore. She was shocked, devastated, and hated her life. Despite everything she did, it was still not enough. She had no energy for herself, she could no longer say she enjoyed the things she did, and she felt abandoned.

Bill's perfectionism was reflected in his perfectly clean car, which he washed every Saturday by hand because he didn't want to scratch it. In it he kept a fresh litter bag, maps, a travel log, and directions to wherever he went, all filed neatly in his glove compartment. He also kept gasoline mileage and service record logs. His garage, jokingly called his "man cave," was spotless. It was a gathering place for the neighbors on his perfect-looking cul-de-sac.

On the job as a car salesman, Bill was the detail person, the one who thought of everything. He worried about what might happen in every situation, offering contingency plans for any eventuality. His work space was extremely organized, and he had special pens and markers for certain types of work. He began each day with a list of "What I Will Do Today," including financial targets, and he honestly expected to do it all. He viewed all of his family, friends, and neighbors as potential customers and went out of his way to do favors, visit, and help with any problem.

He didn't spend much time inside his home. His family complained that he cared more about other people than he did his own family. When Bill came home each day, he walked in the house and scanned the living room and kitchen to see whether it was in order. He commented on and criticized anything that was out of place or any chores that were not done. He felt unappreciated and disrespected if his standards were not met. Tension was rising in his marriage, and eventually his children told him they were afraid of him and his anger. That brought Bill and his family to counseling. He loved his family and was totally unaware of his effect on them. He wanted to change.

Many overt perfectionists keep their homes in perfect order, even if family members refuse to cooperate. With no clutter and no waste, there is a place for everything and everything is in its place. Recycling is most often a must. Schedules may exist for most daily activities: Monday is shopping, Tuesday is ironing, and so on. Even the garbage looks neat when it gets put on the curb. The overt compulsive's physical appearance may be meticulous, though a bit fussy, with a great deal of attention to cleanliness, neatness, the right starch in the shirt, or a perfectly matching scarf with every outfit.

The overt perfectionist looks totally functional and may even serve as a model whom others emulate. Since overt perfectionists are still human beings, after all, it is not unusual for them to appear perfect in one area and out of control in another. They are attempting the impossible and are bound to break down somewhere in their lives. For example, home may be chaotic while work is flawless. Public areas would be the most likely choices for perfectionists to look their best. Overt perfectionists are usually aware of being different from others, sometimes proud of it, but sometimes a bit embarrassed by their compulsive behavior. People joke with them about their controlling natures, and it may be painful to hear, but not enough for them to consider changing. They may have a desire to loosen up but may find it difficult to let go of control. Their issues are very apparent to those around them, who may feel inadequate by comparison or even resentful of the overt perfectionist's air of superiority. Ironically, it is common to find the overt perfectionist surrounded by others who are spontaneous, with no discipline or order. He or she may unconsciously be trying to balance the dynamic in the home.

COVERT PERFECTIONISM

Covert, or "closet," perfectionists are difficult to identify. The compulsion to be perfect is more apparent in their thinking than in specific behaviors. Although they may focus more diligently on one area than another, the nagging thought *I should be perfect* prevails in most areas; however, their actions rarely correlate. They may actually brag about being laid-back and relaxed about life, saying to others, "I don't care what people think of me" or "Life is too short." They fail to verbalize perfectionist thoughts that come too frequently, reflecting self-blame, negative self-talk, defeatist thinking, and in some cases, self-loathing. Self-deprecating humor serves as an effective defense mechanism for their discomfort with personal failings.

Despite the covering up and minimizing, covert perfectionists secretly believe that they should be organized, be caring and attentive to friends, be capable of saying the right thing when called upon, or be better parents, spouses, or workers. They also think they should look better, exercise more, and be in better shape. Covert perfectionists can be their own worst enemies, carrying around an internal, critical parent and waging an invisible battle in the form of intrusive self-talk and constant pressure to be better or "good enough."

On occasion, covert perfectionists may lapse into depression with the slightest failure or misstep, temporarily revealing more outwardly their very high expectations of themselves. In the area of relationships, this type of perfectionism may be a well-kept secret.

In our first counseling session, Linda described herself as a people pleaser. She was thirty-six and divorced, with one child. She was ten minutes late for the session and didn't bring her paperwork, for which she apologized profusely. She had a pleasing personality—smiling, making eye contact, and commenting on the photos and décor in my office. She also had a good sense of humor, which often focused on her own weaknesses, her weight, her clothes, or her need for a haircut. Her reason for coming in was that she struggled with feeling guilty and "bad about herself" much of the time.

When I asked about her life, she said she had three good friends, and she valued her connection with them. At the same time, she was often upset that she was not able to open up or be direct with them. She liked them all, but one in particular was very critical and sometimes judgmental about Linda's choices. This friend was married, was a stay-at-home mom, and had strong opinions that she shared frequently. In this relationship, Linda tried even harder, but she often felt hurt and confused after talking to her friend.

Linda's standards for her role in friendships were extreme. She believed that she should always be in touch, texting or calling several times a day; know instinctively when she was needed; never forget a an important occasion; and never get angry or be selfish or too needy. Even when her friends didn't need anything, she worried that she wasn't doing enough. After a conversation, she would sometimes review things that she said in her mind and wonder if her friend was offended or upset with her. If she did not hear from someone for a while, she would ruminate and worry that she did something wrong. The same dynamic played out in her family relationships. She sometimes found it easier to have no contact at all. Linda felt ashamed of being divorced and blamed herself for not being good enough for her husband.

On several occasions, Linda called a few hours after a session, leaving a phone message apologizing for something she may have said in a counseling session that wasn't right or appropriate.

The personal expectations she had in relationships were so high that eventually Linda started avoiding her friends, but not without guilt, of course. She interpreted this as "They expect too much of me," and she withdrew. Her perfectionism in friendships led to a decision that being alone was better because then she didn't disappoint anyone. Eventually she would try again, but she needed help to do so.

Don was a salesman in the food industry. He had a great personality and was well liked by almost everyone he met. His job was a good fit because of his natural ability to engage people, and they generally remembered him and enjoyed hearing from him. He often compared himself to his peers who relied on systems, schedules, and goals. Don thought that he didn't measure up to them, that he should be more organized and dedicated. Although he frequently outperformed his coworkers, he continued to worry that he wasn't doing enough of the right things to accomplish his financial goals. He was in constant fear of being fired or going broke.

The reality was that he was among the highest performers in the company. He was able to make sales without much effort. Yet he described himself as disorganized, sometimes lazy, and "just plain lucky." Despite appearances, he was waiting to be revealed as the impostor that he believed himself to be. When reflecting on his previous jobs, Don admitted that he preferred to stick to things he knew he could do well. He avoided assignments that would require stretching or learning something new. When offered opportunities for promotion, he declined them. He knew from past experience that when he did extend himself, he approached new tasks so cautiously and with so much self-doubt and criticism that he could not be himself. So he vowed never to take on new opportunities again.

He sought help when he realized that his mental committee of critics was making him miserable whether or not he was successful. He worried and doubted himself no matter what others saw in him.

THE CHARACTERISTICS OF A PERFECTIONIST

Judy and Bill are examples of overt perfectionists, and Linda and Don are examples of covert perfectionists. Let us summarize their possible characteristics and challenges.

Overt Perfectionists

- May be born with a preference for order, but other factors contribute to a lifetime pattern of perfectionism
- Often have a parent with the same inclination
- Are motivated internally by their personal standards and externally by the way others see them
- Have increased anxiety when they don't have order around them, which may appear as frustration, anger, or even rage
- May demand or require that their partners and/or children keep order so that they won't feel anxious or angry
- Are hard on themselves and may be even harder on others
- Tend to be opinionated and like to be right
- May be surrounded by people who are more bothered by their perfectionism than they are
- Tend to avoid participating in a task or an activity that they cannot do very well or understand, often citing that they don't like it or that it's silly (e.g., sports, dancing, music, art, or education)

- Take things they are good at to extremes
- May appear arrogant and judgmental, thinking that they know what is best and that everyone should do it that way
- Fear failure and try to prevent it by being in control

Covert Perfectionists

- May have exceptional gifts and abilities that they are reluctant to pursue
- Compare themselves to overt perfectionists and fall short
- Have low expectations of those around them
- Have high expectations of themselves, which they keep secret
- May exhibit overt perfectionism when they excel at or enjoy a task or an activity
- Prefer being average and under the radar but secretly want to succeed
- Are prone to procrastination, thinking that they must do things right, so they have to wait and do it tomorrow (but not all procrastinators are perfectionists)
- Worry about what others think of them
- Act as chameleons, trying to find the right opinion or the right thing to say to avoid making a mistake
- Underachieve to avoid pressure to succeed or competition with those who are better
- Are inconsistent in achievements and keeping order—despite liking order and success, may reach a point where they have it, then sabotage themselves and fall back into disorder
- Fear both failure and success and will sometimes resign themselves to being average rather than trying and failing

Summary

Although these traits may seem to describe a large segment of the population, not everyone is a perfectionist. Many people have low self-esteem and insecurities, but not all react in this way. The real test is in the belief system and motivation behind the outward behavior. If you are truly exercising choice in a behavior, then it is not perfectionism or any other compulsion. But I believe it is safe to say that if you are reading this book, you probably have some perfectionist tendencies or love someone who does.

This chapter has given the characteristics of two types of perfectionism, but it is not important that you label yourself, if you are not sure. The good news is that once you have identified the overall problem, it is much easier to address it. The solutions are not in the labeling. Perfectionism can't just be willed away by admitting it. Looking deeper is necessary for permanent change.

If you are a family member of a perfectionist, there will be information in Chapter 7 about how to manage the situation.

Chapter
2

The Never-Enough Syndrome: The Origins of Perfectionism

In order to understand how a pattern for perfectionism begins, we must go back to the beginning.

When we are born, we have one task on our agenda: to find our "person," the one who will look into our eyes and transmit the message "I am here for you always." Without this person, we will surely die. Of course, most of us have more than one person who is committed to us—Mom, Dad, Grandma, Aunt, Uncle, Big Sis—but they aren't all committed to us in the same way. We know the difference. If we are really lucky, we may have two people who are that committed to our well-being. The connection we make with this special person is known as *attachment,* a concept that will begin the process of wiring our brains for future relationships.

When we are born, we leave a perfect environment of healthy narcissism and high expectations. I like to call this *plan A.* We believe in perfect love and expect nothing but the unconditional best from others. We are certain that the world outside the womb is waiting for us and will tend to our every need without delay. At the same time, although we don't know it, we are also prepared to deal with human imperfection.

When we come home from the hospital nursery, what a shock it must be to discover that we have siblings or that sometimes we have to wait for a diaper change or to be fed. We may find that there are two adults who don't always get along, that Mom gets migraines, that it is cold sometimes, that grown-ups don't always smile back when we smile, or that siblings can be mean when Mommy isn't watching. We still believe we are the center of the universe, and we don't give up easily.

THE NEED TO ATTACH

Human beings are hardwired to attach; our survival depends on it. Infants are helpless and vulnerable and remain dependent on their caregivers for physical care, safety, and healthy development for many years. Just looking at a newborn helps us to grasp how vulnerable we are. We are unable to hold up our heads, turn over, or communicate what we need. Even after we develop a little more control over our bodies, we are not able to discern what is safe from what will harm us.

What we've come to discover is how critical our early years are, especially from birth to age five, for how our brains are wired in terms of love and connection throughout our lives. For this reason, children will do whatever is necessary for attachment, connection, and attention, regardless of circumstance. With healthy parents who are somewhat capable, the process is less of a struggle, since they are committed to providing what we need, at least most of the time.

We don't need perfect parents, according to respected experts like Donald Winnicott, the attachment researcher who coined the term the *good-enough parent* in 1956.[1] What we do need are parents who are able to nurture and gradually let go of a vulnerable but developing child. It is a tricky balance. Too much attention may be smothering, yet too little can feel abandoning.

THE EFFECT OF FAMILY STRESS ON ATTACHMENT

In the early 1990s, when the first edition of this book was written, there was a great deal of attention paid to the types of dysfunction or stressors a child may have grown up with. The adult children of alcoholics (ACOA) movement was able to make a list of the characteristics shared by those who grew up in families afflicted with alcoholism. Some called it *codependency*, a term also used to describe the characteristics of a spouse or significant other in a relationship with an addict. These hurting adults needed to find a voice and support in order to recover from the damage they had experienced as children, and to fill these needs, a large number of gatherings, conferences, and recovery groups began to form. It was through these groups that the individuals could share their experiences and find answers. The movement was powerful and resulted in the publication of many excellent self-help books. Thus began a time of healing for many.

It appeared, at the time, that the struggles of ACOAs were attributable to the presence of a parent or a partner with an addiction. However, as professionals, we began to notice that many other adults without addiction in their families were struggling in the same ways.

1 Donald W. Winnicott, "Primary Maternal Preoccupation," *Collected Papers: Through Pediatrics to Psychoanalysis* (London: Tavistock, 1958), 300–305.

Over the years, it gradually became evident that the common factor was more likely the disruption in healthy attachment caused by chronic stress in the family. Today we believe that although there may be variable factors—mental illness, addiction, poverty, painful divorce, death of a parent, and so on—in painful families, the interruption of attachment is a universal experience for human beings dealing with stress of any kind early in life.

THE SHIFT FROM PLAN A TO PLAN B: HOW CHILDREN GET WHAT THEY NEED IN STRESSFUL FAMILIES

Once we discover that our connection with our mom or our dad is not as predictable as we had initially hoped when we were born, we look around, and with trial and error we begin to find creative ways to increase the quantity and quality of our contact with our parent(s) through our own efforts. This process may be well on its way by age three. This is what I call *plan B.*

Human beings are pretty amazing and resilient. While our little bodies are developing, our minds are busy reading body language and interpreting facial expressions, touch, and tone of voice in order to figure out what is needed for us to get the attention we must have for survival. When the stress increases and we sense distance from our "person," our anxiety sets off an alarm in our unconscious that propels us toward action. By using a number of variables, we are able to work out the best way to draw in a parent, upstage a sibling, calm the situation, or make someone happy with us. We instinctively experiment with ways to become more comfortable (or soothed), using the least amount of effort necessary.

It is important to note that during adolescence, most of us will shift away from our established pattern and try something new. Don't let this confuse you. You will eventually return to the pattern you developed earlier in life, usually from birth to age seven. Your essence will lead you back to who you really are and how you best manage anxiety in your relationships.

The primary variables involved in the process of adapting to the stress and developing a pattern of managing anxiety include your sex, temperament, personality, and appearance—when combined, your *essence*. Temperament and personality consist of traits like being optimistic, serious, feisty, shy, compassionate, sensitive, easy-going, playful, or creative; having a sense of humor or a tendency to smile or please others; and possessing leadership skills or other natural talents and abilities. These and many other traits are permanent, although we may decide to hide some of them if they are not acceptable to our parent(s). The variables that make up your essence are not good or bad, per se. They become troublesome only when pushed to extremes or when we try to be someone we are not.

Other important variables in developing a pattern of managing the anxiety of insecure attachment are birth order and the choices your older siblings have made before you. Also influential are the events and circumstances that your parents and siblings have experienced before and after you were born, such as the age of your parents when you were born, death, war, crises, infertility, miscarriage, divorce, and illness. We can be deeply affected by things that occurred without our knowledge.

HOW PATTERNS DEVELOP AND CONTINUE INTO OUR ADULT LIVES

I met Julia (age thirty-six) and her husband, Carl (age thirty-five), during a crisis in their marriage. We began by talking about their family histories, and Julia shared information about her relationship with her father that she thought might be relevant. A few years earlier, a family member had revealed to Julia that Julia's father had been married before. She also learned that a child had resulted from that marriage but had died shortly after birth. A divorce soon followed, and Julia's father met and married her mother within a few months. Julia was shocked and saddened by this disclosure and started to question the effect it may have had on her as a child and now as a wife.

Julia recalled that she was never very close to her father. He seemed distant and closed off. When her efforts to reach out to him failed, she assumed that he did not love her or did not want to be close to her. Now, as she faced a similar emotional challenge with her husband, she could not understand why her father would not have shared that information. She blamed herself for not being good enough.

We cannot know for sure how this history affected Julia's life and relationships, but it is safe to assume that her father was deeply hurt by the loss of a child and that it may have been a factor in the lack of attachment Julia felt with him in her early years. She adapted to his distance by being a good girl and trying to make him happy. She was a bright and caring child, and it was in her nature to be compassionate, sensitive, and kind. When she needed to get closer to her parents, she would do something for them or try to please them. Julia learned to help and give love in order to receive the attention she needed. This pattern continued in her friendships and her career.

Now Julia felt alone in her marriage and she was considering divorce. Carl complained that she was never satisfied and seemed irritable and angry toward him. He thought that things were fine when she wasn't criticizing or worrying. Carl was a good and kind man, but he didn't help enough with the responsibilities of home and finances. He stayed away from home as much as he could. He didn't want to face the difficult issues, and Julia couldn't let anything go.

As a perfectionist, Julia was plagued with a lengthy to-do list. She spent her life *doing*, trying to be perfect, and being responsible. She couldn't relax or have fun if there were things that needed to be done. Julia had become the pursuer in her marriage. When she needed love, she asked for help with chores or tried to connect by way of criticism. Carl had a different style and ran from her attempts to connect, which only made her more anxious.

Julia and Carl's pattern is extremely common. It becomes compulsive because it is rooted in and practiced throughout our early development. The pattern may seem complicated and dysfunctional when we are stuck in it. Julia was sure that she was right and Carl was wrong. The fact was that they were both looking in the wrong direction for what they needed. Adults also need attachment, and if a childhood pattern continues undetected, they will use the same pattern with every relationship until they are able to see its futility. Until then, if their method of connecting doesn't work, they just do it more, as irrational as that sounds.

Ron was forty-two when he sought help for what he called "commitment phobia." He was single and claimed to have a good life. He enjoyed his work but wasn't sure it was his true purpose. He dated many women, yet most of his relationships were intense and brief.

He described his pattern as always seeking the perfect partner, particularly in appearance. His relationships were more like interviews for his perfect "person." Once a woman relaxed and reciprocated his affection, he began to doubt his choice and backed away. He felt trapped when he was loved and did not know how to be in love and feel safe. He wanted a lasting relationship, but his actions and his life did not reflect his wish.

In the early stages of his counseling, Ron mentioned casually that he was born after his parents had had seven miscarriages in eight years while using fertility treatments. Several of those miscarriages were late-term. He also had a younger sister. He described his parents' marriage as strained and his mother as loving but "smothering." Mom was extremely supportive and complimentary toward Ron, encouraging him to be whatever he wanted to be and certain that he would eventually find the right person to settle down with. He rarely connected with his father on more than a superficial basis. He had not seen his sister in several years.

Like most adults, Ron did not have memories of his early childhood, but a basic understanding of human nature would suggest that being the first living child after an eight-year struggle would create a somewhat skewed family dynamic. While the situation itself cannot be categorized as merely good or bad, it would certainly have a significant influence on the nature of attachment in the marriage as well as the attachment between parent and child. The grief and fear after years of infertility, disappointment, and loss tend to have a lingering effect that will color the experience of marriage and parenting when a child is finally born.

Through his early childhood, Ron was not aware of the problems that preceded his birth, and he felt very loved and cared for. He did not have a story to explain his current problems. He was not abused, neglected, or traumatized. He was in a traditional family. Sometimes the present is the best clue to our past, however. In Ron's case, his recurring adult problems were based on a long-standing pattern developed early in life. The way we seek attachment and how we attach to others as early as age three are not conscious patterns. They are not based on one event, but rather develop from a long sequence of interactions experienced through the lens of our essence and our environment.

Ron was a cute, easygoing, bright child who quickly developed a sense of what would please his parents, particularly his mother, and get him what he wanted. He found that it was best if he just went along and let his mother feel in control. She was happy when he was happy. When he was away from her, he could do what he wanted and be himself. His mother adored him but did not know him. He needed her love but was often uncomfortable with her control. Ron sometimes sensed that his mother was more attached to him than she was to his father. He described his father as successful but passive and distant, with not much influence over what went on at home. Ron had many superficial friendships without emotional depth. At forty-two, he reported that he had yet to experience a deep connection with anyone.

No single event creates an attachment pattern. Because we need love, we will do whatever is necessary to bring our parents closer to us. We also feel more secure when our parents are connected to each other, so much so that some of us will even try to fix the connection if it seems broken. Ideally, in a low-stress environment, the parents will see that their child needs attention and will provide it even if the child seems difficult, distant, or uninterested.

At twenty-five, Carrie needed help with her conflicts within her family. She described her relationship with her parents and siblings as love-hate. "It's always been this way," she said. "Things go well for a while and then they blow up in my face." The biggest problem was with her mother and her oldest sister. Carrie was the second of four children and never felt good enough for them.

Carrie was born with a feisty personality. She was the child who would ask "Why?" whenever she was told to do something, or she would refuse to cooperate with plans made by her siblings or other children. She had a mind of her own and a voice. Carrie could never understand why her sister and two brothers would just go along with a situation when she knew they didn't like it either. Her sister, Lyn, was obviously her parents' favorite, at least in Carrie's eyes. Carrie was two years younger than Lyn and tended to be hyperactive. Lyn was an "angel" who was sweet and helpful when their parents were around, but she often bullied the other kids when they weren't. No one ever saw her bad side except Carrie.

Carrie's father was an alcoholic, and it seemed to her that Mom turned to Lyn for help and didn't respect Carrie enough to include her. Carrie felt left out, but at the same time, she wasn't sure if she really wanted to get that close to them. Sometimes she just had to say something obnoxious to get noticed. She had a rigid sense of right and wrong and believed that as long as she was telling the truth, she should be able to say what she thought. That used to work for her; it got her some attention and some space, and she didn't care that they were mad at her. Now, however, it was hurting her, and she was afraid of losing her family altogether. Carrie liked her father and thought that he was the only one who "got" her, but he was messed up, too.

When Carrie was born, she needed love and attention as much as everyone else in her family did, but she could not perform as a good little girl on a consistent basis. She was very different from her sister in personality and in her connection to her parents. She was sensitive and outspoken and got more attention in the form of discipline or punishment than as praise. Her sister blamed her for upsetting Mom and Dad, and soon she began to blame herself, too.

Carrie was now living with a roommate and holding a job, but it seemed that she was running into the same conflicts even when she was away from her family. She was also drinking more than she should, which only made her outbursts worse. Her self-worth was lower than ever, and she believed it was all her fault. She was convinced that there was something seriously wrong with her. She couldn't let anyone, especially her sister, know how bad she felt, so she had no support. Love felt like a minefield for Carrie.

Some patterns seem counterproductive in terms of attachment. However crazy they may seem, though, all patterns come from the same place: a desire to be loved. Attachment needs are about feeling a sense of belonging and being seen, touched, known, listened to, and cared about. Some of these needs may be met through negative behavior. We do whatever fits for us and what will work in the context of our world.

In order to grow, Carrie did not have to give up her feisty personality. She just had to learn about her needs as well as the needs of others and to moderate her wonderful need for honesty with everyone at all times. She also had to begin to soften her rigid beliefs in order to be able to accept differences and the boundaries of those she loved.

THE LINGERING CONSEQUENCES OF GROWING UP IN A STRESSFUL OR PAINFUL FAMILY

Family stress can have any number of sources: chemical dependency (probably the cause of the greatest epidemic of family illness in our society), process addictions (such as sex or gambling), mental illness, poverty, physical illness, disability, and so on.

My first book, *Grandchildren of Alcoholics: Another Generation of Co-Dependency* (1988), addresses the multigenerational aspects of painful families. When a family has become acclimated to an identifiable stress such as alcoholism or mental illness, all members of the family will have to develop unique ways to handle the anxiety of inconsistent or insecure attachment over a long period. Remember that this is an unconscious process of using your innate traits and adapting them to the particular situation. The resulting family dynamic becomes the family's "normal."

The children of this family will take into adulthood the skills and attachment styles that were normal for them in childhood and apply them to any relationship or family system they may create, with or without the identifiable stress. This pattern of behavior may continue for generations until it is seen as problematic and help is found.

This adaptation to stressful relationships is not unique to families with severe stress. Over time, many families learn to modify their patterns when the original stress is no longer there. Despite their lack of experience with emotional health in childhood, they may attempt to imitate what they believe is healthy in other families or even from television or movies. They improve some aspects, particularly external behaviors from the previous generation, but they may still have difficulty with relationships, emotions, and self-esteem.

Many perfectionists can relate to having the experience of doing all the right things on the outside yet continuing to struggle with their relationships and sense of self on the inside.

Whereas one generation may have been physically or even sexually abusive, the next generation may adapt and improve by going to the extreme opposite while appearing quite functional. This is what I have called a *looking-good family,* because of its appearance of health, but some very important ingredients of a healthy family are missing. (Chapter 8 will give a complete definition of a healthy family.)

The severity of an individual's struggles depends on many variables. Even within the same family, individuals will have various responses to the stress. Here are some factors to consider:

- The nature and severity of the abuse or neglect
- Birth order and family circumstances at birth
- Outside support systems (such as grandparents or friends)
- Your sex and what that means to this family
- The size of the family—more children than can be cared for, for instance, or an only child
- Environment—poverty, social stigmatization, or racism
- Genetics—which parent you resemble, how you respond to emotional pain, whether your defenses are more or less socially acceptable (as in a perfectionist rather than a rebellious child)
- Your innate survival skills

Not all people, or even siblings, who grow up in dysfunctional families are affected equally. Some individuals who have been exposed to extreme abuse may actually appear to function better than those who have not. My professional experience has been that even though their outward response may be positive, these individuals may still be suffering from emotional pain and low self-esteem. We cannot assume that the person who looks healthy and has a successful career necessarily feels good about any of it.

Emotional neglect is one of the most serious problems in any painful or stressful family. Most parents do the absolute best they can for their children, within the limits of their own upbringing. Despite those efforts, many children have uncertain and inconsistent attachments with their parents and siblings. Good intentions are not a substitute for love. Secure attachment leaves children with a sense of safety, provides them with reassurance in an uncertain world, and helps them to manage their emotions. It reminds them of their value and worth, provides physical affection, and strengthens identity when they are seen as the unique individuals they are. This is a tall order, and no parent can do this job perfectly. That is because they too are human.

Growing up with insecure attachment can have lingering consequences in varying degrees. Here are a few to consider.

An External Locus of Control

Locus of control is a psychological term that describes a person's perceived control over his or her life as either internal or external. Individuals with an internal locus of control tend to believe that they have a high degree of control over their own behavior and the events in their lives. Individuals with an external locus of control tend to believe that other people and outside circumstances have more power to determine the course of their lives.

In painful families where there is insecurity, children begin to depend on people and things outside themselves for comfort, self-worth, and a sense of identity. They develop an external locus of control. Individuals in emotional pain, feeling abandoned and unloved, seek comfort in any form, from people or things. As adults, they look to a lover's reaction to decide whether they are lovable. Without the early reassurance of a healthy attachment, they don't have the "software" for positive or soothing self-talk. They look to others for that.

Adults from painful families show similar signs of emotional dependence in other relationships as well, including at work. Because they have adapted to getting their needs met only occasionally and very inconsistently, they become accustomed to watching and waiting for crumbs of approval to satisfy their emotional needs.

Those who have become accustomed to a life centered on the dysfunction and/or control of others often live as victims of circumstance, waiting for things to change so that they may feel better and get on with life. *Things* may mean a husband's drinking, a mother's illness, a financial crisis, a son's delinquent behavior, a best friend's emotional crisis, the person's own depression, a broken furnace, work pressure, or all of these. These people truly believe that external events are responsible for how they feel.

If they do not have a strong sense of self, they seek validation for their existence and worth from outside. For some, it may come from a relationship. Relationships are entered with the expectation that the love received from a significant other or a friend will make them feel complete and good enough. Those who are career oriented may expect to get approval and a sense of value from a job. They are devastated if the job is lost or if they do not receive the approval they so desperately needed.

Perfectionists are generally future oriented, always planning the next important task or event, always preparing for the next goal. There may be an unconscious expectation that they will be happy when they achieve the goal, but as each thing is accomplished, more is added to the list, and personal satisfaction is rarely attained.

Parents who came from painful families may develop excessive attachments to their children, in a way compensating for their own lack of secure attachment. They then struggle with letting go when their children begin to pull away or when it is important to let go but they can't do it. This issue is prevalent among some parents of addicted or troubled teens or young adults; they continue to hold on, try to fix, and enable, even when it is damaging to all involved. Their difficulties in letting go of their children began with their own insecurities in their childhoods.

Many very successful people, including those in the helping professions, rely on their professions to define who they are. Robert had been a successful salesman for many years, despite having a problem with alcohol. He often thought that his addiction to work (although he didn't define it as an addiction) was more of a concern to his family than his excessive drinking was. He enjoyed living on the edge, never knowing what his income would be or whether he would make it at all. When he was on top, he felt high, motivated to do more. When he didn't make his quota, he was devastated and depressed.

Robert had become dependent on his work for his self-worth and as a way to avoid his feelings, a pattern that continued long into his five-year recovery from alcoholism. A crisis during one of his down periods nearly resulted in a relapse. At that point, he was ready to face his deeper personal issues and sought counseling.

Healthy people with strong self-worth and identity have a solid foundation from which to operate. They enjoy love, approval, and success but do not crumble without it. Their good feelings come from the inside, not from the people and things that surround them. Relying on external people or events for your well-being is like being a runaway kite in the wind.

Repressed Feelings

All human beings have moments when they would prefer to postpone, avoid, and/or deny painful feelings. We are designed to have the ability to do that to a limited extent. Learning to manage emotions is part of growing up, if we are lucky enough to have a parent who has the skill or get help early in life. Many children unfortunately experience frequent emotional pain that is never processed, and for some it is never shared. When that occurs, they must find ways to cope that are generally short-term fixes, and the pain resurfaces in the future.

Today's culture offers many options in terms of methods of covering or forgetting pain, and without help, children and adults will turn to these medicators to feel better. Technology, drugs, alcohol, shopping, gambling, sex, overworking, extreme involvement with sports, busyness, video games, and television are just a few of our favorites. Perfectionists often use workaholism and compulsive busyness as ways of coping. If children are exposed to chronic stress and emotional pain, it will be necessary to find a long-term method of managing their emotions in addition to these self-medicators.

One of the survival skills of family members in pain is to learn to cover up, shut down, disguise, or medicate their own feelings. When they are in pain (which might not be safe to acknowledge in the family of origin), several things may occur:

- They may feel the pain but use masks to cover it. Some use a smile, while others use anger or depression. Internally, they believe the mask to be safer or more acceptable in this family.
- They may deny the pain, telling themselves it isn't that bad and that the situation doesn't really bother them. The pain is then absorbed physically in their bodies, appearing as conditions like low immunity, stomach problems, or pain, or they become depressed or anxious, especially if they are predisposed to that. Children may become aggressive and abusive to siblings or pets and continue that pattern later in life.
- They attempt to repress the entire experience, stepping away from it emotionally. This is called *dissociating*. It may eliminate both the memory and the feelings about it, at least for a while.
- Those who are able to use rational, intellectual means will shut down emotionally and report that they don't feel anything. This too is a temporary fix. They may even lose normal physiological responses, such as a flushing of the face and butterflies in the stomach. Their range of emotions becomes severely limited, and healthy emotional intimacy becomes difficult or impossible.

In a painful family, there may have been generations of adapting by repressing uncomfortable emotions, thereby providing no model of an appropriate expression of feelings.

Nancy, a client in her mid-fifties, reported that her mother suffered from bipolar disorder throughout Nancy's childhood. She had extreme mood swings in which she would be charming at one time and violent at another. Nancy was a very bright little girl who adapted to this emotional chaos by reading her mother's signals and responding accordingly. She came to believe that anger meant rage and that sadness meant months of depression. She was determined not to lose control, as her mother had.

Since Nancy was very intelligent, she began to use her mind to figure things out, stay in control of her emotions, and get approval. She got wonderful grades and functioned exceptionally well until she began dating and attempted to have a relationship. It was in that context that Nancy said she felt emotionally illiterate. She did not feel what other people felt and could not be open emotionally. She did not know what was missing in her life until a desire for intimacy led her to reach out for help.

Comfort with Crisis Leads to Reenactments

Growing up with stress creates a feeling of normalcy in it, and we can become unaware of its effects. Childhood role models may foster the assumption that life really is crazy and demonstrate that the children need not be concerned when things appear out of control to others. Thus they have normalized stress.

Some people unconsciously try to quiet or minimize their emotional pain. Those, like me, who have a tendency toward hyperactivity and seem to prefer tasks and activities to people, will find that chaos or a major challenge provides a convenient distraction when they would prefer not to dwell on the problems and feelings in their lives. They develop the belief that once they finish their tasks—something that never happens—they will settle down to relax and feel.

One of the most extreme examples I have ever come across was a former client named Barbara, who was twenty-eight but appeared to be much older. She was beginning counseling because she believed it would help her mother, whom she described as a caretaker. Barbara's father was an alcoholic, and he and her mother had recently separated. Barbara was her mother's "best friend" and sole emotional support. She took her mother to Al-Anon meetings because Mom was afraid to drive, and when they were together, Barbara listened endlessly to her mother's detailed stories about her alcoholic father.

Barbara claimed to be detached from her mother because she had a busy life of her own. She lived in an apartment with a roommate who was physically disabled by multiple sclerosis. Barbara took on the responsibility of driving her roommate to work, shopping, and providing companionship for her. Barbara was a caseworker in the county welfare department and was excellent in her job, showing great compassion and patience with other people's misfortune.

Barbara was not aware of the crisis in her own life because she stayed focused on the lives of others. Only in group counseling, when she was away from those she cared for, could she get in touch with the burdens of her childhood and her own grief for the neglect to which she had become so accustomed. When she talked about her circumstances with her group, she was able to see her own pain reflected back to her in the faces of her peers.

An overfunctioning pattern is more typically seen in those who use the distraction around them to minimize or avoid pain. Options are always available and can include caretaking; volunteering; taking on most of the responsibility at home, at work, and in relationships; or inventing ways to fill time (e.g., decorating, entertaining, or coaching). Healthy relationships and family life require quality and quantity of time and attention. Chaos prevents that.

Difficulty Regulating Emotions in Close Relationships

Depending on the pattern we develop in childhood and the degree of insecurity we experience in our attachments, most of us will exhibit one of the following four styles in our closest relationships:[2]

1. **Secure attachment style.** With secure attachment, we are able to move in and out of connection with others, seeking comfort and responding to others who need comfort. We experience and express a range of positive and negative emotions and are willing and able to allow others to do the same.
2. **Anxious attachment style.** This describes those whose anxiety increases significantly when they feel separated or disconnected from someone they care about. For the anxiously attached individual, the only thing that will decrease anxiety is to reconnect in a positive way with that person. Anxiously attached people may pursue with questions, hoping for answers that will help them to calm down. If that doesn't work, they may mentally try to figure out what is wrong and come up with causes and solutions. Their anxiety is triggered further if the loved one won't communicate. They feel unable to let go and may overstep the boundaries of others in their desperation to lessen their pain. It is important for those with this pattern to learn ways to manage their anxiety, fear, and pain when they experience distance in their relationships. An extreme overreaction to a minor slight may be a clue to childhood attachment injuries that are unresolved. The pain is then easily triggered and difficult to resolve until it is dealt with.

2 Susan M. Johnson, *Becoming an Emotionally Focused Couples Therapist: The Workbook* (New York: Routledge, Taylor and Francis Group, 2005).

3. **Avoidant attachment style.** In this style, the tendency is to manage anxiety by keeping a distance and thereby avoiding conflict and distress. Introverts with this style may be isolated and occupy themselves with solitary activities and work. Extraverts with this style prefer to be around many people and yet lack emotional depth in their relationships. Both tend to be self-sufficient and busy with tasks and obligations when opportunities arise for closeness. They may appear as "moving targets" to those who love them and seek connection. Individuals with this pattern are often very sensitive and cannot tolerate emotional intensity, whether it is love or anger. They are not fully aware of their pattern and may blame a dysfunctional partner for the lack of closeness in the relationship. As long as they are with someone who doesn't have the ability to be intimate, they will not see their own inability to attach in a healthy way.
4. **Fearful-avoidant attachment style.** In this style, an individual may avoid intimacy by withholding commitment and enjoying only brief but intense relationships. Many people, similar to Ron in the example above, will alternate between fear of abandonment and fear of entrapment. When anxiety and mistrust inevitably arise, these people run from love entirely or search once again for the perfect soul mate who will make them want to stay and break the cycle. A perfectionist with this pattern may spend a lifetime in search of the one who will make him or her whole. Unless the individual develops the awareness of the fear and develops the ability to give and receive comfort from a partner, he or she will be forever dissatisfied or alone.

Isolation and Lack of Support

Without secure attachment, many adults from painful or stressful families will have assumed that the world is not a safe place, that people cannot be trusted, and that it is much wiser to take care of oneself than to be set up for disappointment and hurt. They also believe that they cannot depend on their own perceptions to be accurate. As a result, in order to avoid humiliation and hurt, they keep things to themselves. Some individuals with an outgoing, pleasing temperament may develop excellent social skills and be surrounded by people, but they will nevertheless be isolated internally and truly not known by others.

With chronic feelings of insecurity, any sign of rejection can feel like a "near death" experience. Reactions to disapproval or criticism are blown out of proportion, resulting in chronic mood swings and failed relationships.

In many families, isolation is reinforced by rules such as "Don't tell anyone family business," "We can do it alone," or "Don't ask for help outside the family." Siblings in painful families often disclose that although they witnessed the same painful incidents in the family, they were not able to talk about them even with one another, much less with anyone outside the family. Many report having conversations decades later in which they ask a sibling, "Did you see that?" about something that happened when they were very young.

The feeling of isolation is something I experienced personally. Although I was not consciously aware of it, I grew up with a feeling that I did not belong. I was a middle child, and even though my friends seemed to like me and I thought my family loved me, I had the sense that none of them really knew me. Despite the fact that

I talked quite a bit and could socialize on a superficial level, I was afraid and unable to open up and reveal my feelings or thoughts to anyone. In truth, I didn't know how I felt or what I thought. I became a chameleon of sorts.

I felt very alone and paid close attention to what seemed to be the right things to do in order to be accepted. This contributed greatly to my growing perfectionism. I believed that if I didn't make any mistakes in my relationships, I would belong and be accepted. Of course, it was impossible to avoid making mistakes by saying or doing the wrong thing, and I was secretly devastated with any sign of disapproval or criticism. When my mistake was pointed out, I felt worthless and unlovable. I kept that pain to myself and vowed to try harder, to be more vigilant, and to reveal myself less and less over time. This continued until I was an adult. I was exhausted, overworked, and had relationships with primarily underfunctioning people. Because such self-vigilance is impossible to maintain, I found myself avoiding my family and friends, preferring work over close relationships. With professional help, I learned that what was holding me back was fear of abandonment and shame. I believed I was defective and never good enough.

Summary

This chapter explained why we have patterns of behavior that seem to be somewhat unconscious and repetitive. The reason we are not able to change on our own is that a pattern is not simply a habit. It is a way of coping that used to serve a purpose but that it is now getting in the way of quality living. Insecure attachment in childhood is at the root of many compulsive patterns.

The important message here is that the pattern of perfectionism is a normal and necessary adaptation that is not dysfunctional or bad. Any child in a stressful or painful family would have to adapt in order to maintain a connection with a parent. Each of us finds our own individual way of adapting, depending on temperament, birth order, sibling choices, and other circumstances. All patterns are necessary and have a purpose. When a pattern starts to become a problem as an adult, it may need to be modified. To do that, you need to know yourself and your pattern very well.

Chapter 3

Who Are the Perfectionists?

It may be difficult for you to see yourself honestly. In this chapter we'll look at some ways to find out more about your pattern.

SELF-TESTS

This list is a guide to help you determine the degree of perfectionism in yourself. Most people have a few positive responses, but if you check three or more items on two out of three tests, this may be a serious issue for you to look at.

There are three tests. Test 1 is general, test 2 is for possible overts, and test 3 is for possible coverts. Complete the first one and then take either the second or the third—or both, if you aren't sure.

Test 1: General

- I place excessive demands on myself.
- I often obsess about the details of a task, even though they may not be important.

- I have trouble letting go of something once I have finished it (e.g., a project, a writing assignment, a paint job, a letter, taxes, or a cleanup job).
- I get very upset with myself when I make a mistake.
- I get more upset when I make a mistake and someone sees it.
- I often have a mental list of things I "should" be doing.
- I never seem to be doing enough.
- I tend to notice any error in myself or others before I notice the positive.
- I am very upset by criticism.
- I get defensive when I am corrected or criticized.
- I have difficulty making decisions.
- I get upset if I have to learn something new and I don't catch on quickly.

Test 2: Overts

- I rarely make mistakes.
- I tend to criticize or complain about the way other people do things.
- People say I am too "together" (e.g., uptight or neat).
- I am annoyed when others don't act or behave as well as I think they should (e.g., in being on time or keeping order).
- Others would describe me as a perfectionist.
- My surroundings are generally in good order.
- I feel frustrated when my home is cluttered.
- I prefer routine and structure.
- I am very organized in one or more areas of my life.
- I sometimes wish I could just let go and relax.

- I have an all-or-nothing philosophy: If I can't do it all, or do it well, why bother?
- I am sometimes hard on the people around me.

Test 3: Coverts

- I procrastinate on tasks that require a lot of effort.
- I am very hard on myself when I make mistakes.
- I feel terrible when anyone sees me make a mistake.
- I consider myself to be laid-back.
- I am critical of myself in my head.
- I think a lot about what I should be doing.
- I don't usually measure up to what I think I should be.
- I am not interested in being the best at most things.
- When I am good at something, I try harder.
- I tend to avoid things that I may not be good at.
- I often believe that people don't think highly of me.
- Others say that I am better than I think of myself.
- I underestimate my abilities at many things.

INDICATORS OF PERFECTIONISM

To better understand the specific things you or someone you know is struggling with, a list of indicators and how they affect life is given below.

Avoiding Stillness and Quiet

The negative self-talk we become so accustomed to makes it difficult for us to enjoy moments of peace. Some have described those critical voices as the "committee." They tell us we aren't doing enough or that we are stupid. The criticism goes on and on; it is an endless cycle. When we stop our compulsive behavior, we are haunted with unexplained feelings of guilt, shame, anger, hurt, or fear.

As a college student, I studied in a student lounge filled with conversation and smoke while I played pinochle and listened to music. It was a joke among my friends that I would easily break any campus record for the fewest hours spent in the library. I could not concentrate when it was quiet because the "committee" was in session. I was a covert perfectionist who was afraid to try, and I was certain I would never have grades as good as my peers or my siblings had.

Many of us use frenetic activity to distract us. We bustle around the house or the office at a constant pace, with the television or the radio on to drown out our thoughts.

I interviewed Dan about his perfectionism, and this is how he described his lifelong pattern. He was twelve years old when he took a job as a short-order cook in an extremely busy fast-food restaurant. He dedicated himself to becoming the best at his job. "We used to serve 140 people in thirty minutes," he explained. "I could remember eight or nine orders in my mind, and then somebody would ask for a check and I would add it up in my head—including the tax—while I took care of what was cooking and someone else was talking to me."

As the child of two alcoholic parents, Dan found great comfort and distraction in his work and his accomplishments, but this method of avoiding pain worked only while he was busy. As soon as he stopped working, the voices of inadequacy and worry would begin. As he got older, he found that overworking and being the best at whatever he was doing was the only way he could stay calm and comfortable. After he also began to use drugs and alcohol when he wasn't working, he knew that he had to learn to face his thoughts and feelings to find peace.

This need for intensity can affect one's career choice. We may choose a stressful and chaotic job over a slower-paced but more enjoyable one. It also causes us to overlook problems in our personal lives. We could solve or prevent problems, but instead we tolerate or ignore bad situations and procrastinate on solutions. Feelings from the past also make it impossible to let go of the intensity.

After college, I chose to work in a detox unit—in a very rough part of town—counseling addicts who lived on the street. I enjoyed a job that many people quit after one week or less. At the time, I also had serious problems in my personal life that I could not face. My success at work helped me to forget those problems and delay decisions I would eventually have to make. Work became the one place where I felt good about myself.

Emotional health and personal growth require slowing down the mental chatter so that feelings can come to the surface. Many people need help to recognize what they feel and manage their emotions in a more effective way. We will look more closely at how to do that later in the book.

Placing Excessive Demands on Time and Energy, yet Never Doing Enough

Perfectionists frequently set themselves up to fail with the fatal to-do list. They function as though someone were standing over them with a whip saying, "Do more, do more!"

On a typical Saturday, after having worked forty or more hours during the week, Les, one of my interviewees, would rise at 8:00 AM, thinking he should have been up earlier. This is the list he would look at first thing in the morning:

- Clean garage

- Take Mom to the mall
- Cut the grass
- Fix bathroom sink
- Take watch to be fixed
- Get Joan a birthday present
- Help Todd rotate tires
- Iron clothes

Around 3:30 PM, Les would realize he had not played ball with his son or talked to his wife and that he would not finish what he had planned for the day. Another day off had been blown. At this point, he began to feel worthless and inadequate because he did not do enough. He felt very tired, but he ignored it, since he had so much more to do. This was his typical Saturday. For him, every weekend felt like the film *Groundhog Day,* in which a disgruntled TV weatherman (Bill Murray) finds himself waking up to the task of covering Groundhog Day with Punxsutawney Phil again and again.

When he walked around his house and his yard, Les could see only what he had not yet done. Every project called out to him. No matter what he did, it wasn't enough. The list he created would carry over to Sunday, with a few more items added. He vowed to do the rest on weeknights but never could. He left himself no time for contact with himself or his loved ones. This was time reserved for when the list was finished.

Many perfectionists play victim to the clock, believing that if only there were more time, they would get everything done. The fact is, we never will. The things we put off as "unimportant" are items like intimacy, parenting, fun, and exercise. We intend to get to these things but rarely do. We may even feel guilty and inadequate about not playing enough. The voice of the old "committee" continues to say, "Never enough, never enough!" Ignoring our own bodies and physical limitations as well as our need for connection with those we love prevents us from tuning in to what we really need and want. This eventually leads to isolation and possibly depression and illness.

Obsessing Over the Details of a Task and Making It Bigger Than Life

The most anxiety-producing thing I ever experienced was the anticipation of writing my first book. Other people worry about the term paper that will be due at the end of the semester, the speech they are giving in five months, the house that needs remodeling, the taxes that have to be done, the new job they will be seeking next year, and on and on. When we have anxiety, it is always about the future: something that is not happening now is going to happen.

My thoughts about writing at the time were focused on what people would think about it—how it would be received by my family, my publisher, my peers, and anyone who would read it. I was terrified that it wouldn't be good enough or that I would reveal more than I should. And all this was before I had even written a word! I was anxious enough to give myself a migraine headache and an upset stomach just by thinking. Fortunately, I reached out for help and worked through it, and as long as I stayed in the moment while writing, I actually enjoyed it. I am doing that right now as I work on this book. I really like to write, and I'm grateful that I get to do it.

Perfectionists believe that they must do the anticipated project perfectly to avoid any unforeseen problems in the future. They start to worry about it before they have even begun. Acting as though the entire project were in front of them at that very moment causes them to feel incapable of doing it. This may lead to procrastination. Perfectionists are unable to break a project down into manageable parts and may make such a catastrophe of it that it finally looks impossible.

Many people experience a physical response to their thoughts—such as nausea, a pounding heart, a cold sweat, or diarrhea—at the mere thought of beginning. As a result, they tend to avoid anything that arouses anxiety while they wait for the fear to go away.

Candy shared her experience. "When I was younger," she said, "I never attempted to do anything if there was a chance I might fail. Failure was not allowed in my home. If I had a challenge ahead of me, like a test, I would think about it with dread and terror months or weeks in advance. If there was a way to avoid it, I would. Often, I would end up so scared that I would put it off until the last minute and cram the night before an exam. I would still do well, but I couldn't take credit for it. I quit college halfway through and never went back because of my perfectionism."

Many adults spend years wanting to go to college, but they put it off while they wait to feel confident about it. They may have struggled with high school when they were immature and troubled, and they assume college will be the same. Adults are different from teenagers and can do anything they set their minds to, if they put one foot in front of the other, one moment at a time. If the goal is perfection or nothing, adults will have irrational thinking and will do nothing. The belief that they have to do it perfectly is compounded by the obsession with the details and possible problems. The result is procrastination and indecision.

Perfectionists who do achieve a desired goal may still drive themselves crazy in the process. They tend to overprepare, compare themselves to others who have done similar work, redo until they are totally satisfied, argue over grades, and worry every step of the way. In the end, they often say, "It could have been better."

Being Frustrated With and Criticizing the Imperfections of Others

The internal, critical voice that perfectionists use on themselves is also projected onto others, applying the same impossibly high standards of performance that they cannot meet to those with whom they relate. Perfectionists may feel angry and frustrated with everyday human error, such as lateness, sloppy housekeeping, poor manners, bad driving, incorrect word usage, or shoddy work. They often criticize qualities that they themselves have. The anxiety that they deny having about their own vulnerabilities pours out when they see flaws in others, and the mistakes of others create disorder and thus anxiety in the perfectionist, who has no way to calm it but by changing something external.

Melanie said, "I really can't stand to hear a grammatical error—at least when I'm listening to a lecture or a presentation or sometimes even in casual conversation, and I get terribly distracted when reading if I see a mistake. In fact, I sometimes get angry at the writer, and if there are a number of errors, I might even stop reading the item entirely." It is no surprise to discover that Melanie had perfectionist parents who were also critical and pointed out every error in anything she said or wrote. I'm certain that despite a great deal of editing, there will still be errors in this book. Sorry about that—I hope you keep reading.

Jean was frequently told by her friends and her family that she seemed angry and impatient most of the time. Before she began counseling and reading self-help books, she was extremely difficult to work with. As a nursing supervisor, she focused consistently on the mistakes of her employees. She believed that if she wanted something done right, she had to do it herself. Her performance evaluations pointed out her excessive need for control and her lack of confidence in her staff.

Since Jean believed that she worked harder and better than everyone else, she could not accept this feedback. She blamed her supervisor for not understanding her difficult situation. She felt overworked and unappreciated and was upset with her supervisor for not accepting her employee evaluations as constructive criticism.

At home, Jean was also very critical with her children. When looking at a school paper with her son, she would immediately see a flaw and comment on it. She found herself treating her kids in much the same way she had been treated as a child, and she became frightened by it. She had vowed early in her life that she would never do what her parents did to her.

In counseling, Jean discovered that the way she viewed others was a reflection of what she felt about herself. In a way, this focus on the flaws of others allowed her to avoid her own. In reality, she believed that she was worthless and should be perfect. Her children had become an extension of herself, and they had to be perfect for her to feel adequate and appear to be an adequate parent. This belief had to change before she could be more accepting of others.

The characteristic of being critical of others can be extremely damaging to people close to the perfectionist. It is especially difficult when we exercise authority, such as being a parent or a supervisor. It may also cause isolation: people avoid telling the perfectionist anything or asking for something because the result will be painful and make things worse.

Practicing Rigid, Purposeless Rituals in the Name of Organization, Structure, Cleanliness, or the Right Way

Here are a few brief examples of what perfectionists have shared with me:

- In his work life, Tom made extensive lists for every task. He drew columns and lines on each page in a special notebook, putting little boxes before each line to be checked off later. It took him precious time each day to do this. He felt great when he checked things off and was also teaching his child to use that method.
- Janet was married to an alcoholic. Although she described her life as totally unmanageable, her house was always in perfect order. She vacuumed every room every day until members of her support group finally told her that she didn't need to do this. Giving it up was not easy. Doing so meant having idle time to feel her pain.
- A certain perfectionist described her father's orderliness at home this way: "My dad was a genius, the vice president of a major corporation. When he was at home, he would relax by working in his workshop. His tools were always arranged from the largest to the smallest: screwdrivers, hammers, socket wrenches—all arranged the same way. He built cabinets that held perfectly arranged sets of drill bits and special racks that held perfectly arranged grades of sandpaper. A special closet held labeled and numbered cans of paint, varnish, and wood stain. The closet door held an array of perfectly displayed paintbrushes, from the tiniest camel hair brush to a five-inch-wide brush. These brushes were also arranged

according to their composition and the type of job they were purchased for. When the firemen came for a voluntary yearly inspection, they were always amazed at our basement. Nothing was ever out of place. When my dad died, I realized that I never really knew him."

Other examples of perfectionist rituals are as follows:

- Ironing underwear and sheets
- Waxing the car weekly (not because it needs it, but because you are "supposed" to)
- Washing dresser drawers and inside cabinets twice a year
- Sending thank-you notes for cards received on your birthday
- Planning in detail any excursion from home, even shopping, and declining any invitation with short notice
- Spending hours organizing activities but only minutes doing them

Many of these things do not pose a problem at face value. In fact, others may even admire a person who has such discipline. The difficulty begins when things like intimacy, relaxation, and time with children take a backseat to the need for order and when the organizing and cleaning have become a method for handling emotional pain.

Feeling Inadequate, Guilty, and Shameful When Our Humanness Shows

Perfectionists operate from the belief that they should be perfect, then they beat themselves up whenever they fall short. This is often quite extreme in one area of life but hardly visible in another.

Although Ed appeared to be a laid-back sort of guy, he judged himself harshly in his relationships. He had the expectation that he should never cause displeasure for those he loved. In therapy, Ed described this frequent scenario: After an encounter with a family member or a friend, he would find himself mentally reviewing everything he had said and done, looking for the flaws in his behavior. He would then begin to feel guilty for some slight comment he *may* have made, which he thought *might* have been insensitive or hurtful.

All of this would take place in his head, with no evidence that the other person was actually upset or hurt. Ed's feelings of guilt would grow until they no longer were about his behavior but were a reflection of his worth as a person. This stronger, deeper pain is called *shame.*

At this point Ed would feel bad, worthless, and unlovable. After hours or days of emotional turmoil, Ed would call the person he believed he had offended and apologize. The supposed victim of his error usually did not recall the event and had not been offended in the least. Once forgiven, Ed would feel better, vowing never to make such an error again. This is something that is, unfortunately, humanly impossible. It never occurred to him that his thinking might be flawed or that he might be overreacting because of childhood pain that was triggered by these incidents.

Amy wrote, "I hate to fail. It isn't that I made a mistake or that something didn't work out, it's that I am a failure. Even if I've never done something before, if I fail, I'm devastated. I can beat myself up for months because of a mistake. Either that, or I try to convince myself that it doesn't matter, and I have a hard time taking a risk and trying that activity or similar activities again."

A woman at a lecture on perfectionism commented, "I had a job once, a job I really didn't like, and I was told by my supervisor that this job was not working out for me. I burst into tears in my boss's office, sobbing. I had never failed at anything before or received negative feedback like that. Rather than look at how I could improve or make changes and rationally come to a decision about the job, I quit immediately. For weeks after that, I couldn't sleep without having dreams about failing. That incident hurt me so badly that it finally brought me to therapy." This was another example of how paralyzing shame can be. When a perfectionist has spent her life making very few mistakes and one finally occurs, she is devastated and unprepared.

Competing Mentally or Behaviorally in Any Endeavor

We all know people who appear to be extremely competitive in many areas of their lives. They are often seen as determined, ambitious, energetic, or even driven to win. In some areas of life, the overt perfectionist may feel the need to be the best and yet never feel satisfied with the outcome. Upon winning, a small voice in his or her mind says something like the following:

- "My partner wasn't very good—that's why I won at racquetball."
- "I only got an A because we weren't tested on anything I didn't study."
- "I got the promotion, but I really don't deserve it. If the boss finds out who I really am, I'll be fired."
- "I may be very successful, but what about the other guy who does so much more, makes more money, and is smarter?"
- "My wife says I'm a great lover, but she's probably faking."
- "What have I done lately?"

The point is that even those who look the best struggle with these negative voices. They have the notion that in order to feel okay, they must be better than others. Jan, for example, was talented at almost everything she attempted. But she confided, "I find it hard now to see myself as okay and acceptable as I am. I feel like I have to earn acceptance from others by doing all things well in order to feel good about myself. I know that underneath it, I feel shame. I've become very preoccupied with my tennis lately, playing an hour and a half each morning. I do it to feel good, but then I get very upset at myself when I miss a shot that I have made before. The bad feeling lingers through the day. I've done this with other sports, too. I take the fun and the benefits out of it."

Covert perfectionists are also competitive, but it is experienced more internally. They may expend much energy observing the successes of others, believing that they should have the same gifts, abilities, and accomplishments. They may jokingly comment on how noncompetitive they are, while internally they are critically evaluating themselves in comparison to others.

One covert perfectionist had this to say about the mental anguish of believing you should be the best: "In my academic work, I spent years simply avoiding anything at which I thought I might not be outstanding. This meant that I sold myself short and deprived myself of years of learning and experiences that might have been exciting, rather than risk being mediocre."

Although she graduated 8th in a class of 360, she still believed it was not good enough.

Perfectionists may also become extremely uncomfortable when a spouse, a coworker, or a friend experiences success, loses weight, gets an award, or just feels great. They feel inadequate and "less than" the other person and are often unable to celebrate the success of someone they love without feeling bad about themselves.

Having an All-or-Nothing Approach to Life

The perfectionist uses terms (mentally, if not verbally) such as *right* or *wrong, always* or *never,* or *good* or *bad* and says the word *should* as often as possible. These terms reflect the belief that there is always a correct way to think and be. Truth, of course, is often relative, determined by an individual at a particular time and place and given a specific set of circumstances. People's views are as numerous as the stars in the sky. Nonetheless, perfectionists believe they must find the right way, behave that way, and convince others to do the same.

Here are some examples of this kind of thinking:

- People should always be on time.
- In an argument, it is essential to determine who is right and who is wrong. You must convince the other person that your way is right, and you should not give up until he or she agrees.
- An activity shared with another person, like a movie, a television program, or a concert, is either good or bad. We should agree on our perceptions of that experience. If we don't, there is something wrong with you.
- There is a proper way to drive a car, talk to others, dress, and work. If you or I do not perform this way, we are at fault.

Perfectionist students may silently harbor the belief that they should know everything there is to know about a particular subject before taking a test or submitting a paper. I remember thinking that I should have read every book on alcoholism cover to cover before writing my master's thesis. Even though I received an A, I secretly believed that my paper wasn't as good as it should have been.

When confronted with this thinking pattern, most perfectionists would acknowledge that it is neither realistic nor possible to be perfectly correct or thorough. But because we operate from low self-worth and emotional pain, we may believe that others are capable and that we are just not as good. This is a compulsive, irrational pattern of thinking.

Struggling with Spirituality and Feeling Unworthy and Judged

The term *spirituality* implies an emotional, intimate connection both with something greater than us and with our own internal spirit. The "something greater" may be God and religion, but it also may be a very strong belief in any group or concept, such as love, the earth, the universe, or fellowship. For some, it suggests a need for or a dependence on God or others for something we do not have alone.

The connection with one's inner spirit is often related to developing a sense of who we are and who we were meant to be. This connection is without judgment and is one of love and appreciation for oneself. Spirituality and perfectionism are contradictory; instead of reaching for a higher power or God, the perfectionist is trying to be God, all-knowing and all-powerful.

Perfectionists operate from the belief that they will be accepted by God, themselves, or others only after they have achieved a perfect state. Any attempt at spiritual connection will be focused on performing a ritual, fulfilling a duty, and seeking approval rather than having an instinctive, intuitive desire to reach beyond human limitation to something more meaningful.

Lorraine described how her strict religious upbringing coupled with her perfectionism made it very difficult for her to rely on a loving God. "My religious training as a child convinced me that I had to be perfect," she said. "After all, God was keeping track of all my actions. I found it particularly disconcerting when I had to go to confession. I feared for lack of acceptance from God, so I usually did a lot of rationalizing to keep from having to confess a mortal sin. Because of my understanding of the Last Judgment, I expected to find myself sitting in a giant movie theater, with the entire world watching, as all my transgressions passed across the screen. It never occurred to me that God might be more interested in the good things I had done rather than the bad."

A child's experience of living in a painful family and having difficulties with the most significant authority figures in life, one's parents, alters the perceptions of a higher power and makes it impossible to accept that anyone could or would love us unconditionally. Spiritual growth is easier if we face our disappointments, fears, and lack of trust with parents, preferably in counseling before we attempt total surrender to a higher power.

TAKING THE FAST TRACK TO PERSONAL GROWTH OR RECOVERY

There are many circumstances that prompt an individual to make a major life change. Chemical dependency and other compulsive behaviors, depression, parenting concerns, and basic relationship issues are all very common motivators. Regardless of the impetus for entering a process of personal growth, the perfectionist, once motivated, will jump in with both feet. The shame intrinsic to perfectionism will create a need to get well fast and to do it right.

Sam was the child of two alcoholic parents and was chemically dependent himself. When he began his recovery, he did everything he was asked to do by members of his Alcoholics Anonymous group. Before very long, he had a sponsor, was working the twelve steps exactly as he had been directed, and began to do some service work as well. Sam went to meetings seven days a week, meditated daily, and even read numerous books on the subject. After eight months, he relapsed. Why?

Like Sam, many perfectionists in recovery change their behavior and language long before they actually begin the internal process that is required for lasting results. They have spent a lifetime avoiding their shame by doing and performing. In recovery, they quickly catch on to the expectations of their group, their therapist, and their peers. They know how to look good. Unfortunately, their feelings may not change, and this will inevitably sabotage all of their efforts to do their recovery perfectly.

Here are some warning signs of perfectionism as you grow and change:

- Becoming overly zealous in learning all there is to know about yourself and your family. You may find yourself looking feverishly for a simple explanation for everything that is wrong with you. You will never learn it all. Experts will never know it all, either.
- Trying too hard to be the perfect client, doing all the assignments, and joining a twelve-step group or group therapy for support. Perhaps you think you don't belong there because you aren't as desperate as the others seem to be. You may even find yourself reorganizing the meeting format, the literature,

or the coffee setup. Service and helping out is important, but perfectionists may begin to turn a support system into a problem.

- Maintaining, even in a support group or a therapy group, a looking-good image. Learning the language, slogans, and jargon of self-help books or support groups and becoming too well too fast only serves to convince others that you don't need anything. Before you know it, either you are surrounded by others who need you or you're alone and unapproachable.
- Comparing yourself to others who began before you, or even with you, and actually competing for wellness. Each of us works at an individual pace, and the time it will take depends on personal history along with many other factors.
- Expecting perfect consistency on your path. Believing that you should never slide back into your old ways.
- Losing control of yourself or overworking. All of us do these things some of the time.
- Minimizing progress while making a list of your defects that need work. On any day, we can choose to look at how far we've come or at how far we need to go. Perfectionists in recovery need to focus on their essence and not on their accomplishments. Becoming vulnerable and authentic takes honesty and time.
- Attempting to fix one's family so that it too will be healthy. Our energy needs to be spent on changing ourselves and being supportive of others as they make their own choices. It's better to model what you are learning than to talk about it.
- Parenting with perfection. Moving too quickly, out of shame, to fix our children and repair all the damage done in the past.

Reading books, reciting affirmations, and pushing them to share feelings does not work as well as just changing yourself and modeling health. Others may not trust your behavioral change and may need to see and experience it over time. Selling it doesn't work well and often creates new problems. Children need love and acceptance.

- Seeking perfection as a long-term goal in life. Some of us continue to harbor the belief that if we do this right, we will be free of painful emotions, character defects, and our history forever. Even if this is believed at an unconscious level, it will frustrate us as we struggle to accept ourselves as we are, one day at a time. Perfectionism in the process of personal growth is inevitable if this has been a lifetime pattern.

Summary

Not all perfectionists are the same. Where in life perfectionism appears to be a problem is very individual. Many people suffer from perfectionism in their relationships. Others would say that work is the most uncomfortable place for them. Parents may be full of self-doubt about their parenting decisions. Both men and women struggle with critical thoughts about their appearance or their health.

Some have a pattern of criticizing those around them, even those they love, or they need to have perfect order in their environment to find peace. For some of us, the pattern of perfectionism is visible for all to see; for others it is primarily in their minds. The feelings of anxiety, shame, and guilt that drive this behavior are similar for all perfectionists, although the outward appearances may be vastly different.

Chapter 4

The Price of Perfection

When I speak publicly about perfectionism, audiences are quite receptive and even entertained by the subject. The humor with which we approach the topic is in part a reflection of our minimization of its severity. I believe that humor can help perfectionists when they are trying to find balance; however, we also need to take a serious look at the personal costs of ignoring the issue. Our families and friends may tease us about it, and we may feel a bit irritated by it, but is it really all that big a deal?

The negative side of the story is the price we pay for our perfectionism. I have drawn this chapter from the shared experiences of those I surveyed and interviewed as well as from the comments and stories of many workshop participants.

THE SURVEY

Because I was questioning only perfectionists, it was not unusual for people to critique the survey while they completed it. Most were not comfortable responding with a simple yes or no and chose to write explanations for their answers instead. Some even attached letters, giving me input on how I might have done it better. (Yes, I used some of their suggestions!)

Survey Results

I surveyed 126 people who identified themselves as possible perfectionists. This group may have consisted of mainly overt perfectionists, since most coverts don't recognize the issue as easily. The respondents were 70 percent women and 30 percent men. I am certain that men suffer from perfectionism just as much as women do, but my source of participants was primarily the human service network and personal growth workshops, which tend to draw mostly women. Of the respondents, 33 percent were recovering from chemical dependency.

Regarding family history, 94 percent reported a moderate to severely dysfunctional family of origin; 46 percent reported having a perfectionist parent, and 45 percent (with some overlap) reported a workaholic parent. It is very common for an individual to be a perfectionist and also a workaholic. Both are often reinforced as acceptable and even desirable compulsions in our society. Of those surveyed, 50 percent were firstborn children.

Men and women showed differences in descriptions of their own perfectionism. All of the men and 47 percent of the women listed work as the number-one area affected. The remaining 53 percent of women listed the following number-one areas, in this order of frequency: parenting, physical appearance, household responsibilities, relationships, sex, and health.

The majority of those surveyed thought that the people around them were moderately to severely affected by their perfectionism.

They listed the following as problematic in relationships, in this order of frequency: control issues, lack of intimacy and shared feelings, a gap between the emotional health levels of the partners (i.e., one party was getting help with issues and the other was not), and communication.

Health problems were listed for 95 percent. Some described very serious stress-related conditions; others reported chronic but less severe problems. Asked to list their most serious health problems, the participants listed them in this order of frequency: headaches, sleep disturbance, digestive problems, back pain, overeating, sexual dysfunction, and chest pain.

Interpersonal difficulties with procrastination, decision making, depression, and even suicidal thoughts were listed by the majority of those surveyed. Decision making was listed as problematic for 70 percent; several answered "sometimes" when asked, "Do you have difficulty making decisions?"

Upon making a decision, 75 percent said they struggle with doubts afterward, 58 percent reported occasional suicidal thoughts, and a few had attempted suicide in the past. This figure is not unlike any report about clients in counseling, who frequently reach such depths of depression that they may momentarily view suicide as the only way out. It is also consistent with other research on perfectionism.

Asked how often they actually achieve perfection, 10 percent answered "frequently," 50 percent responded "once in a while," and 40 percent marked "never." This indicates that the majority of perfectionists have some success—or at least believe they do—in the pursuit of perfection.

Your Values

Before we start looking at the negative consequences, I would like you to get a clear picture of what you really want and value in your life. Below I have listed the things I hear from clients and most adults when they are asked what they value and want to enhance in their lives. One way to think of it would be to ask yourself, *If I had only one year to live, what would be important to me?*

I have organized the values according to the area of life they relate to. When you look over this list, check those that matter most to you. You can then create a list for yourself that you may want to post in a visible place in your home.

Individual Values

These pertain just to you.

- Feel peace of mind
- Feel emotionally secure—that I am okay
- Feel gratitude for who I am and what I have
- Have quiet time for myself
- Have faith in something more than myself
- View myself as a kind, compassionate person
- Find and use my gifts
- Give something back
- Enjoy life, have fun, and play
- Take risks to do and learn new things
- Have a loving relationship
- Be a loving person
- Be real—let my vulnerability show
- Take care of myself
- Be physically healthy
- Be at home in my body
- Keep learning and growing

Relationship Values

These pertain to family and friends.

- Have regular, positive contact with my family of origin
- Tell people that I love them
- Make my relationships a priority
- Share my vulnerabilities with those I love
- Have at least two or three good friends
- Be able to say no when I need to
- Have fun and adventure
- Show up for others when it is important
- Ask for what I need

Intimate Relationships

Complete this whether or not you have an intimate partner.

- Be equal
- Be interdependent
- Know that feelings are more important than stuff (chores, money, or work)
- Listen to my partner
- Validate myself and my partner
- Be open and honest about who I am and what I need
- Give and receive affection every day
- Be comfortable with sexuality in the relationship
- Be vulnerable—real and authentic
- Show up for myself and my partner when it matters—no excuses
- Be generous
- Be committed no matter what
- Share successes, dreams, and painful times

- Accept my partner as he or she is
- Be accepted as I am

Family Life and Children

- Accept others as they are, with unconditional love
- Get to know my children
- Spend quality time with the people I love
- Guide my children to be themselves and provide the tools for that to happen
- Maintain a consistent healthy connection, contact, or attachment
- Smile, make eye contact, say hello and good-bye
- Create a strong parental bond in terms of love and decision making
- Have fun and adventure
- Allow for differences in each individual
- Give reassurance when needed
- Create a space where vulnerability is encouraged and respected by all
- Create a structure that supports love in the home
- Balance work and play
- Provide a sense of safety and protection

Work, Career, or School

- Support my values and choices financially
- Have it fit with who I am—my essence, gifts, and talents
- Balance it well with my personal life
- Work in a setting that fits well with my family life and my personality

- Be paid what I am worth
- Ask respectfully for what I need
- Be able to participate in my family life and do my work
- Learn something new
- Try new things
- Focus on doing my best because it pleases me, not because I have to
- Be proud and grateful for what I contribute
- Make a difference in the world
- Like the people I work with

I did not choose to write values that I think are "good," the "best," or the "right" ones to have. Be sure you are not choosing the ones you think you "should" have. Your list must reflect what matters to you deep down inside. Remember: If you had one year to live, what would be important to you?

After you have spent time with this list, add things that may be important to you that are not on it. This will be your personal list, not a mandate for anyone else in your life. The goal is for you to begin to have your life be a reflection of what you truly value. If you can do that, others may follow you. We do not have the right to dictate someone else's values.

THE NEGATIVE CONSEQUENCES OF PERFECTIONISM

As with any compulsive behavior, there is a pattern of progression, the consequences become more serious over time, and deterioration appears in more areas of life. The areas most often reported as damaged are work, parenting, relationships, and health and body image.

Overachievement at Work or in School

In my own life, work was the area most affected by my perfectionism. There I was an overt perfectionist; at home and in my relationships, I was more covert. Like many perfectionists, I found work that was a great fit and that I enjoyed. At the age of twenty-three, I began to get all of my self-worth from my career. This was in contrast to my personal life, which seemed to be out of my hands. I felt some control and value in the workplace, even though I was a very low-paid and unappreciated counselor.

One thing I've always known how to do is work hard. Even when I was a waitress during high school and college, I had to be the best waitress. In the detox unit, I felt responsible for everything: washing clothes for someone who had been living under a bridge for a month, serving good-quality food, designing a good program, or helping a person stay sober. My personal life was totally unmanageable at the time, but I knew what I was doing when I went to work.

Ironically, I was being paid for only one-third of the duties I assumed were mine. I could not understand why I was not appreciated or compensated for what I did. In hindsight, I realize that I must have been impossible to deal with as an employee. I was extremely critical of anyone who did not do things as well as I did or who did not totally agree with me. I resented authority. I was a workaholic who had a hard time understanding people who simply worked to earn money.

My peers today will find this hard to believe, but eventually I was fired for swearing at my boss and telling him what to do. I may have been technically right in what I said—he *was* incompetent—but that doesn't count much when you're unemployed and a single parent.

After that experience, I decided that I knew how such programs should be done and began to develop some of my own. I did some fine work, but I did most of it alone for a few years. I believed that no one could do it as well as I could. At one point, I had sixty outpatient clients, ran four evening therapy groups per week, and was a program director. People admired my ability to do everything, and they let me.

After years of performing that way, I had the benefit of training experiences and eventually a support group and therapy that provided insight into my life and my pattern. I started to look more closely at my personal life. Today I have learned to operate as part of a team and to delegate to and seek help from others. I truly love it this way. It works well only when I am willing to be vulnerable, honor my feelings, and tend to my personal life. Perfectionism and workaholism were handy tools to help me avoid my personal life. They don't work for me anymore.

The word *work* means many things, depending on one's lifestyle or stage of development. As children, and often in adult life as well, perfectionists exercise their compulsive behavior in school. Sandy remembers vividly trying to be Little Miss Perfect. "I was nine years old and I was teaching the Palmer method [a painfully perfect method of cursive handwriting with precise arm movements taught during the 1950s] in a Catholic school," she recalled. "I was put in charge when the nun would leave the room. I couldn't have any friends, because I was a miniature teacher." Sandy needed the praise and even enjoyed it, but she was aware of the isolation that resulted from being too good.

For many, achievement in school was the only way to gain attention and approval from parents. One young man discovered the unpredictability of such approval and described it this way: "My father, who had quite literally ignored me for the first sixteen years of my life, finally noticed me when I got nearly perfect SAT scores. Suddenly, this man who never talked to me about school realized that I might get into any college and spent all his time that summer driving me to every Ivy League school on the East Coast. It was very uncomfortable for me."

Mary said, "As a child I always wanted to do what was asked of me. At school, I was quiet and sat at my desk with my hands folded in front of me. I was fearful of authority figures and at the same time wanted their approval. I remember my penmanship class and how very careful I was to be as perfect and neat as possible. In my early teen years, my notebooks were orderly and neat, and my drawings of lab specimens were nicely labeled—I used colors to make them look better."

Mary's pattern continued into adulthood. "I sought out more work and responsibility," she explained, "and no matter what I did, I still felt like it was never enough. My papers and writings were neat, and my work areas were clean and organized. I was once told that I worked so rapidly that I appeared to be mechanically producing great volumes of work and not thinking about what I was doing. I always had the sense that if I learned enough things, I would be worthy to be alive."

> ***REFLECTION:*** If you relate to any of the above examples, take a look at your values and make a note about what adjustments you may need to make. A good thing to look at is your primary motivation for doing the work and also for how you do it. If change is needed, think of it as a slow, long-term shift, and if possible, try a more spiritual approach to finding what is best for you and your loved ones.

Never-Ending Household Responsibilities

A perfectionist's home can seem full of nagging ghosts that haunt day and night, saying, "Remember me? I'm the dirty closet you haven't cleaned in two years!" No home can ever be perfect. If the people have children and make them a priority, the home won't even come close to being perfect—but there still may be the expectation that it should.

Perfectionists look at designer homes on television, in movies, and in magazines and expect theirs to be the same. Sandy, a successful businesswoman, said, "When I saw a picture in a magazine, that was how I thought my home was supposed to be. It may have taken a photographer five days to arrange that shot for one picture, but I would think, *Oh, so that's the way a house is supposed to look*—that when you open the door, you're supposed to look like a movie star opening the door to this perfect house, with the perfect car in the drive, and the fresh flowers in the entry, perfectly arranged."

Many couples seem to act out their feelings of inadequacy or their discontent in their relationships through organizing, cleaning, and fixing their homes. They may feel a chronic compulsion to fix things up or take care of landscaping as though they were in a competition. They feel great for a little while after something is accomplished, but then the list is always updated, and they are disappointed in themselves again. Their personal relationship becomes centered on tasks, and the romance and intimacy get put on the back burner.

If they are unable to do what they believe are necessary projects, some people resort to all-or-nothing: they surrender and live in total disorder. They think, *If I can't do it right, why bother?* If things get out of hand, a covert perfectionist may not allow anyone into the house, feeling embarrassed and more inadequate, even restricting the children from having friends over. Covert perfectionists may have a messy house as a result of the hectic lives they lead, but they secretly believe that until it is perfect, they will never be okay.

A perfect house doesn't prove the worth of the person or people in it. It may even point to a lack of balance and demonstrate priorities that are out of sync with one's value system. A home should, above all, be about love. If it is possible to have both love and neatness, that's great. Perfection and love don't coexist very well. Remember that it isn't the house that is the problem; it is your own thoughts about the house and the choices you made that created the stress.

When perfectionists are anxious, they begin to fix the world around them to get order in their minds. When they live with other people, they may demand that their roommates, children, or partners help to create order. Perfectionists become critical partners or parents, expecting those they love to help reduce their anxiety by being perfect, too. Relationships and families are often destroyed by this dynamic.

REFLECTION: Has your house or apartment become more important than the people in it? Again, review your values around relationships and work. See how they measure up to the reality of what is on your mind, how long the to-do list has become, and when you last shared a quiet moment with the people you love. Are things more important than people in your life? If so, your relationships are suffering. If you have let things go, are you sitting around cursing yourself, or are you making yourself and your relationships better and stronger with the extra time you have? Covert perfectionists can delegate and energize a team of family and friends to get acceptable order into the chaos around them.

Fear of Criticism in the Workplace

Perfectionists avoid and do everything possible to prevent criticism, rejection, disapproval, abandonment, or being fired. Some will concentrate on never making a mistake; others will stay under the radar. Some are careful to stay in their own areas of expertise and not take risks. My favorite way to avoid being criticized was to do more than anyone else, get things in before they were due, and never say no to a request. It worked fairly well, but I suffered from stress-related health issues (chronic migraines) and carried my stress home to my family.

Erin was an administrative assistant in a law office, a job she performed flawlessly and alone. Her only difficulty came with her tendency to make decisions independently, without checking them out with her coworkers. She spent much of her energy trying to avoid criticism and had to avoid people in the process.

When Erin was evaluated, her boss had many positive comments about the quantity of work she performed and her strong personal commitment. But he also commented on her isolation.

Characteristically, Erin distorted her feedback and heard only one thing: "You make bad decisions; people don't like you." She did not hear the rest of her evaluation. At first, Erin felt embarrassed, then ashamed, and finally—an hour later—she was furious. She believed she was unappreciated and should quit.

Erin always expected that her boss would catch her making a mistake and fire her. She worried constantly about not doing enough or missing something. Whenever the boss asked to see her, she cringed, feeling sure that this was the end. It never occurred to her that admitting she did not know something and asking for help would probably greatly enhance her performance and keep her employed.

Erin had been through this before at other jobs. Her solution was to leave before her employers found out any more about her and start fresh in another workplace. She blamed each employer for expecting too much and not thanking her enough. The latest experience felt familiar, and Erin knew she had to address her own insecurities.

> ***REFLECTION:*** In today's human resources environment, most of us will have to experience appraisals. Feedback is a valuable thing, especially if you respect your boss's opinion and want to grow. Without feedback or input from *people* (i.e., outside your own head), you learn very little. When you know what needs adjusting, you can say thanks and work on it. If you are getting only positive feedback, it may be that people see you as fragile and unable to handle criticism or that you are arrogant and defensive, which only causes conflict. If your values list includes learning and growing, you may want to look at how you handle feedback.

Fear of Success and the Inability to Enjoy It

Perfectionists are often very successful at what they do, in terms of status achieved or financial gains. They start out believing that the reason they don't feel okay is that they have not done enough. Once they arrive at an identified goal (e.g., a certain salary, a promotion, graduation, or being published), they expect to feel better, so they work harder, better, and longer than anyone else. Once they have met the initial goal, however, they have to set a new goal they must achieve in order to be okay again.

When I wrote my first book, a dream I had had since childhood, I expected to feel elated and satisfied with my accomplishment. But instead, I felt very detached from what I had done. I could not own it. I read the words and could not imagine that they came from me. In order to appreciate and be thankful that I had done it, I asked my friends to help me and even threw a party to celebrate. It helped a lot—until time passed. Then I noticed that my professional peers had written more than one book—in fact, more than two—and I began to minimize what I had done. In writing my second book, I worked on enjoying the process instead of striving for the goal.

Another challenge for some perfectionists is that they have a degree of internal pressure that is intolerable even before they start a project. They expect that if they do accomplish something significant, they won't be able to repeat it, yet people will expect them to be successful all the time in all areas of life. Some fear the visibility, exposure, and criticism that may come if they succeed. They will be compared to others, which will then trigger shame.

REFLECTION: If you value learning new things, using your gifts, and being yourself, it is important to practice mindfulness (i.e., staying in the present). When you are in this moment, anything is possible. Say to yourself, *It isn't happening now*, and take the next right step in the direction of your goal or dream.

Unattainable Standards in Parenting

Being the child of a perfectionist is extremely difficult. Judy had two perfectionist parents and described it this way: "The problem with having perfectionist parents is that they are very inconsistent in their demands. I never knew what I was supposed to be perfect at and what didn't matter. The perfectionism in my family is selective and therefore very confusing. If my parents wanted to do something (or wanted it done), they expected it to be perfect. If it was a task that they didn't care about, it didn't matter how it was done.

"Often," she continued, "they gave me the tasks that they didn't like and expected perfection from me on the tasks that they would do carelessly. They were never satisfied with anything I did. It wasn't good enough."

The fact is that perfectionism in parenting does not make sense. From the child's perspective, it is hurtful, unfair, and unreasonable. Children know instinctively that it is impossible to be perfect. What is expected of them may even be beyond their reach developmentally.

Judy recalled this painful memory: "I remember my father asking me to do something for him, like go get a tool. He would very abruptly give me an order, expecting that I had all the information he did. I did not know one tool from another, even if he had told me before. When I would come back with the wrong one, he'd call me stupid and scream at me. Then I couldn't think at all, and I'd make more mistakes. The more he expected of me, the less I could perform. The anxiety about making a mistake started to make me sick. I'd get stomachaches and headaches all the time."

It would not be natural for a child under the age of about twelve to be capable of cleaning a bedroom to the point of perfection. In fact, a parent might have reason for concern about OCD. It is not normal for children to do dishes, make beds, wash the car, vacuum, or dust as well as an adult. They don't see what adults see and have shorter attention spans. It is also useless to suggest to children that there is actually a "right" way to do anything. Soon they grow up, go out into the world, and find out that there are thousands of "right" and "better" ways.

If they have been raised by controlling perfectionists, teenagers haven't learned to think for themselves, so they keep looking for the rule book to guide them, or they avoid anything that might be challenging. One client, role-playing in group therapy, faced her "family members" in a childlike manner and demanded plaintively, "Just tell me what I'm supposed to do, and I'll do it!" They had been telling her what to do for years, and she kept waiting for their approval, which never came. As she grew up, she used the same approach with anyone she dealt with, whether at school or at work. She was a very good person, able and willing to do what was expected; but the rules kept changing and the rewards never came. She felt lost and angry.

The children of perfectionists often grow up without realizing there was anything wrong and thus parent their children the same way they were parented. Even those who hated what was done to them tend to repeat the family pattern. It is also common for adults who grew up in chaos to decide to do the opposite with their own children. These perfectionists go to the extreme of "perfect" parenting. A few people I interviewed were so determined to be perfect parents that they made a choice to remain childless. Since some perfectionists also reported having difficulty making decisions, many put off having children out of fear until it was too late.

The concept of looking-good families was a focus of my first book, *Grandchildren of Alcoholics*, in which I described the dynamics of a family with at least one perfectionist parent. Quite often, the motivation for a parent trying so hard to do it right is an unconscious attempt to overcome a painful family history and to show *their* parents and the world how it should be done. They do this in the hope that their parents will approve of them if it turns out well, and it also serves to create external order out of internal disorder. The need to control people and things to prevent mistakes serves as a way of managing emotions and is a driving force when perfectionists have children.

Attempts to control family dynamics, children, or life events are doomed to fail. The perfectionist parent, when feeling anxious and out of control, simply exerts more control and attempts to create order to ease his or her fears. The parent's anxiety is then passed on to the family.

Examples of such control are the following:

- **Rigid order.** Everything has a proper place (or at least the belongings of the perfectionist do).
- **Cleanliness.** This is more important than life, relationships, fun, or being a child. "Don't get dirty." "Work first, play later."
- **Much planning but little action.** Everything must be planned and is therefore too much trouble.
- **"What will the neighbors think?"** Children must look, talk, and act perfectly, or Mom and Dad will look bad.
- **Fun becomes work.** Playing, whether in sports, music, or board games, must be done as well as possible. Children must always strive to do it better, longer, and faster than before. Flaws are pointed out and suggestions made for improvement.
- **Striving for excellence.** Always do your best, especially at school, where others will notice. For some, the hidden message is that a child should accomplish what his or her parents couldn't do.
- **Anxiety about sickness.** Some families obsess about health issues, dressing right for the weather, taking a child's temperature frequently, keeping a child away from friends who may have germs, or force-feeding vegetables and vitamins. The parents' anxiety is passed on to the children.
- **"Eat right so that I'll feel like a good mother."** The parent (usually the mother) decides if and when the child is hungry.

Older children must ask if they can have a drink or a cookie. Food intake is controlled and dictated.

Perfectionist parents rely on these external controls to try to gain a sense of internal comfort. They do not intend to abuse their children. In fact, they believe they are creating the best possible environment in which to prepare their children for the world. The fault is in trying too hard. The anxiety that is behind that effort creates fear in a child, which may last a lifetime.

If parents have a need to be perfect, family togetherness becomes enmeshment. There is no space, privacy, or individual identity. An anxious desire to be close to one's children may lead to the crossing of healthy boundaries. A parent's decision to have an active family, whether through sports, travel, or other activities, may be forced upon the children and feel intrusive if their interests aren't included in the decision making.

Children raised in such a rigid atmosphere are so smothered and controlled that they often have no choice but to rebel. Being defiant, sick, or sloppy; getting poor grades; or just refusing to cooperate are almost necessary tools for survival. Some children with compliant personalities will grow up to be perfectionist parents themselves.

Leanne, who grew up with a perfectionist mother, wrote, "At 6:00 AM I would practice piano for a half hour, and my sister would then do the same. I believed that if only I was good enough, Dad would stop drinking and Mom would be happier. If I complained, Mom would cry. So I just tried to be the best little girl I could be. My younger sister didn't comply the way I did. She left as soon as she could and, ironically, they liked her better."

REFLECTION: Healthy parenting is not about what we tell our children to do or how to be; it is about who we are as role models. When you parent from your values, you have a better chance of doing a good job. Overuse of the word *should* will sabotage your efforts if it is based on an external standard of perfection rather than values. Try to substitute the word *could.* Good parents make many mistakes, but love and acceptance balances the scale.

Unattainable Standards in Relationships

If you have seen only dysfunction in your family relationships, you probably look at television shows, at other families, at the neighbors, or at friends and assume that there really are perfect relationships. I would agree that there are people and couples who *look* perfect, but no one actually *is* perfect. All relationships are made up of imperfect human beings with needs, problems, feelings, and flaws. They are also surrounded by other human beings who are equally flawed. There are some very healthy but imperfect relationships as well, which we will explore in Chapter 9.

Many perfectionists do not consider their relationships to be seriously affected by their habits when most of their compulsivity is expressed in their work. This lack of awareness is a relationship problem in itself. It takes time, commitment, and dedication to maintain a relationship. Workaholics and perfectionists are stretched to the limit and have little time and energy to devote to it.

How does perfectionism affect our relationships? The participants in my survey said that the areas of greatest difficulty for them were control issues, lack of intimacy and shared feelings, a gap between the emotional health levels of the partners, and communication.

The Need for Control

People who come from dysfunctional families often believe that control means safety. Being in control means having a predictable life in which nothing happens that you can't handle; your friend or your lover thinks like you, does things the way you do them, meets your needs (without being asked), and expresses feelings, but only the ones you want to hear. Of course, when we ourselves are asked to perform this way, we know how impossible it is.

Control, like perfection, is an illusion. The few moments you think you have it are probably just the people in your life letting you believe it for a while, hoping you'll stop trying to achieve it. Controlling is an act of fear, an attempt to manage our own anxiety by fixing or changing other people. Why would anyone want the responsibility for directing the rest of the world? There is one understandable rationale, but it is still flawed thinking: If I cannot manage my anxiety when others around me are struggling, I must hurry up and fix what is wrong in them so I can feel calm and secure again. The thinking is flawed because fixing and changing others is actually impossible. They also don't like it and will sabotage your efforts every chance they get.

Dictating or even just obsessing about how others should live, feel, act, talk, or dress serves to alienate them, forcing them to pretend that they agree with you rather than being genuinely themselves. When you attempt to control or offer unwanted help to another adult, you are indirectly saying, "You aren't good enough the way you are. I can't trust you to make good judgments or to not upset me." If it happens to be someone close to you, you might also be concerned that people will think badly of you if the person you're trying to control makes a mistake.

Here is the challenge for a perfectionist: If you are honest with yourself about your motivation and accept it as truth, you will then have to learn how to manage your anxiety when people around you are making mistakes, instead of asking them to change. We will look at how to do that later on.

There are moments in our lives—in a crisis situation, for example—when it is wise to take control; this is a choice. Compulsive controlling is not by choice. Most people don't even know they are anxious and will jump into fixing without thought. That behavior is an attempt to gain safety by altering the outside world, including a primary relationship, to fit our needs. Since true feelings of safety come from within, this method does not work and often serves to destroy the relationship. People who are controlling are also subject to being controlled because they are other-directed and not mindful of their own feelings. Lack of self-awareness gives others an advantage, since they know your weaknesses better than you do.

> ***REFLECTION:*** Ask yourself how your life would change if you woke up tomorrow and accepted everyone in your life as they are. Isn't that exactly what you want others to do for you? Letting go of expectations and judgments of those you love is a gift to yourself and to them. You are free of the responsibility of making others happy, and they are free to make choices and learn from their experiences.

The challenge for you is to learn to manage your anxiety and disease when others are struggling with their own problems. The solution is to look inside yourself and develop a new way of facing your fears and calming anxious thoughts without imposing them on those you love or care about.

Lack of Intimacy and Shared Feelings

We learn intimacy and the expression of feelings from our parents. Adults from painful families did not have a role model to teach them about managing emotions. Perfectionism compounds the problem further. Perfectionists put a great deal of effort into work, tasks, activities, and appearances; however, very little effort is put into the area of emotional attachment where they do not feel as competent. In friendships, for example, perfectionists may believe that a good friend does the following:

- Always remembers birthdays, sends a card, and takes the other person out to dinner
- Knows instinctively when the other person needs something and then provides it
- Says "Thank you" and returns the favor whenever the other person has done something for the friend
- Shows interest in the other person's family and enjoys it as much as the other person does
- Texts daily, talks to the other person on the phone at least twice a week, and is available whenever the other person needs to talk, no matter what the friend is doing
- Helps with chores like painting or fixing something and is available whenever asked
- Invites the other person to any gatherings or parties the friend may have

Granted, these sound a bit extreme, but perfectionists often harbor these secret notions and feel inadequate when they do not honor them. Some also expect the same in return and are deeply hurt if their generosity isn't reciprocated. Covert perfectionists can be plagued with guilt and anxiety over their performance in friendships and sibling relationships.

With their significant other, the perfectionist feels that a good husband, wife, or lover should always do the following:

- Have sex when the partner wants to, even if one is tired
- Listen to the partner talk about work for as long as the partner needs
- Understand when the partner doesn't have the energy to parent, help around the house, or listen
- Respect the need for space, even when one needs to talk to the partner

All of the above items are focused on doing the right things to be a perfect partner in a relationship. We often pick up these ideas from reading books or watching TV or movies, or maybe these are really what we expect and wish others to do for us. They are very nice, but none of them have anything to do with intimacy, and holding these expectations is a setup for feeling like a failure. It is simply impossible to be that good. Covert perfectionists may feel internal pressure to perform this way but believe they are not good enough. Overt perfectionists will try to be the perfect partner but still fall short.

Even if many of these gestures of love are lacking, the relationship could still be intimate and healthy. Intimacy has to do with an honest emotional connection between two adults and does not require selfless adoration. Chapter 5 will address the ingredients more specifically.

Perfectionism in a relationship is a deterrent to intimacy. Intimacy requires that we let go and allow ourselves to be vulnerable, with no idea of the outcome. There will be love and there will be conflict. The active perfectionist cannot do this because he or she cannot predict the outcome. The difficulty with hiding or suppressing feelings is that you lose the ability to choose which ones to hide, and you lose love and closeness in the process.

REFLECTION: Look once again at your values list. If you want peace more than you want closeness and openness, avoiding conflict is the way to go. It takes courage to be vulnerable and to listen to the emotions of a loved one. It takes practice and sometimes professional help to learn to do it. If you value being known and knowing your partner, you will find it rewarding to give up trying to be good and perfect.

A Gap Between the Emotional Health Levels of the Partners

When an individual begins a process of personal growth, it is often with the hope that it will change others. After all, that's what perfectionism is about. It can be very disappointing to find out that a spouse or a lover is not interested in joining you on your journey and, in fact, may be going in a different direction. It can be painful when you first become aware that you are growing apart, and it's hard to accept that your loved one may not join you in your struggles and successes.

The good news is that emotional health is more attractive than perfectionism, but it takes time for others to see it. If a relationship is important to you, counseling may be needed to build a bridge between you. In Chapter 7, I will make suggestions about how to handle yourself when you begin to change and others don't.

Making significant changes in the way we conduct a relationship means letting go of desired results. This isn't a short-term process. It may or may not be in the plan for us to continue the relationship we are in. Once self-esteem starts to improve, many people raise their relationships standards. The values list is an example of that.

Over time, you may feel that you don't know the person you live with, or that the "you" who made that choice has changed. With a lot of effort, it is possible for a couple to start over and build a healthier relationship. It will be just as difficult to end this relationship and start over with someone new. Whatever your pattern has been in past relationships, you will still be the same person, but you will have new abilities to be honest, assertive, vulnerable, and direct.

REFLECTION: The common denominator in every problem you have is *you*. We bring ourselves and our history with us, and we may repeat destructive patterns many times before we truly change. Perfectionists tend to expect perfection and sameness in a partner. Your partner will find his or her own path, and it will surely be different from yours.

Perfectionists often want easy solutions they can think through and implement. This is not an easily resolved area. As you change, it is important to focus on yourself, trusting that you will be okay no matter what. That can even relieve some of the pressure to control and may improve things. Spouses, friends, and children each need to make their own choices about life and cannot be forced into changing because we think it's a good idea. This is an area in which less is more. The less we do to force solutions, the quicker and easier they will come.

Communication

Many overt perfectionists believe there is a right way to communicate. If they tend to be more intellectual, using logic and remaining rational at all times, they may be more concerned with staying in control than with the message they are giving. It is true that we say more with our body language than with our words. We can be speaking perfectly, calmly, and succinctly, yet be expressing rage toward the person we are talking to. It is very common for a logical person to be matched up with an emotionally expressive partner.

The perfectionist may out-talk the emotional person, using reason and logic. This approach, which some perfectionists would view as superior, leaves the partner feeling negated and impotent but with no recourse, since the argument was so sound. Contrary to many opinions, perfect word usage and logic do not constitute healthy communication in intimate relationships. Close relationships require emotional honesty, validation, empathetic listening, and time. Problems develop when we deny having feelings or try to hide our fears and other feelings behind our words.

Regardless of style, the attitudes and behaviors below may be present when a perfectionist attempts to communicate:

1. Someone is right and someone is wrong. You must convince the other person that you are right and why, until the other person concedes or feels foolish for disagreeing. Whether you use logic or drama, you may end up right and alone.
2. Opinions must be supported with logic and proof that they are correct. Feelings don't count if they don't make sense to you or if they make you look bad.
3. Wearing your opponents down with logic or drama until they lose control of themselves will make you feel superior and possibly prove your point.
4. Continually deflecting and focusing on the faults of the other person so that no one will notice yours means that you won't have to look at your own shortcomings.

5. Hiding your shame by acting superior. A good perfectionist will express others' feelings and thoughts for them.

Covert perfectionists may communicate by not talking because they have convinced themselves that they can't do it right. They expect to be overpowered and lose every argument. (They too believe that winning is the goal, but they can't compete with logic.) They then feel ashamed and stupid for not expressing themselves.

> ***REFLECTION:*** Steven Covey has said, "Begin with the end in mind."[1] In other words, what do you value most when you communicate? What is the goal? When we use communication to protect and defend ourselves more than to share who we are, it is no wonder that our relationships and our self-esteem suffer. We also forget that half of communicating is listening and doing our best to hear and understand what is being said.

Health and Body Image

Messages about the need for physical perfection are all around us, such as the following:

- Botox is the way to take ten years off your face.
- At age seventy-four, Jane Fonda looks forty; so can you.
- Special formulas can prevent hair loss, because it's bad to allow nature to run its course.

Our desire to fix our outsides and to soothe our insides, combined with our competitive nature, pushes us to have the perfect body and to be in perfect health. We should look as good as any friend who is

1 Steven R. Covey, *Seven Habits of Highly Effective People: Power Lessons in Personal Change* (New York: Simon and Schuster, 2004), 95.

in shape or the model or celebrity in a magazine. Of course, we rarely achieve this standard, and even those who come close are never quite good enough, always striving for more and more.

Recent health crazes include being constantly aware of cholesterol level, blood pressure, calories, and the environmental hazards of cell phones and water bottles. It all seems pretty positive and harmless until it is put in the hands of a perfectionist. As the constant flow of information increases the pressure to be perfect, perfectionists respond with alarm. The problem is not in what we are doing or not doing, but in our motivation and the degree of intensity applied to the task. I would love to see the following slogan run across the television screen when one of these self-improvement products is advertised: Chronic anxiety and perfectionism can have adverse effects on your health. Lighten up!

REFLECTION: The tendency of the perfectionist is to flip from one extreme to the other, all in an effort to avoid painful feelings, particularly shame. If we focus our recovery on who we are at this moment rather than on who we should be, working on self-acceptance more than self-improvement, our outsides will start to show results. If one of your personal values is to feel at peace and okay, you'll find it easier to take good care of yourself when you've reached the decision that you truly are okay as you are right now, this minute.

Summary

This chapter was based on a survey of people who were willing to share their experiences and their specific areas of concern. I added the section on identifying values so that you may view your quality of life through the lens of the things you value and the goals you have for your life. There is no right way to be. If you are aligned with your values, there is no need to change. If you feel out of alignment, this is a place to begin.

The information in this chapter highlighted the negative consequences of perfectionism. As you read, it may be hard to admit that you have some of these issues, and your shame may be increasing. The goal of this book is self-acceptance, not more self-judgment and criticism. To achieve this, it is important to view it from a larger, family perspective in order to understand that we did not get this way alone, and we don't have to work through it alone.

Chapter
5

How Did I Get to Be So Good?

This is an exciting time to be a therapist. I admit that my knowledge of neuroscience is minimal, but I make up for it in curiosity and enthusiasm for the information steadily coming in from research on the brain and emotions. This research confirms and validates what we have observed and come to believe about human beings and their emotional processes. Therapists now have the benefit of the advances in attachment theory and brain science to enhance and validate our work.

We have always assumed that much of what human beings consider to be challenges or gifts is a product of the temperament or personality that we were born with. We also know that environment helps to shape and balance these inborn traits. This is true whether we grew up in a healthy family or a very painful one. When we have the overlay of chronic stress and emotional pain, some of our natural characteristics become compulsive. For example, a positive trait like a pleasing personality (e.g., a born smiler) may turn into attempts to gain approval and connection by pretending to be happy all the time. If a trait must be overused to improve our chances of having a secure attachment with our parents and others, it will often go too far and become a problem later in life.

There is no doubt that one's future is influenced and shaped by one's family background. Clients I have worked with often have a narrow vision of how this works. Most tend to focus on how their parents directly interacted with them as individuals. They fail to factor in the circumstances surrounding them as a family and rarely consider the effect of things that occurred before they or even their parents were born. Since each parent also brings an emotional legacy into the family, a client cannot look at only one generation to examine the effects. Without help, children in pain become adults in pain, but they learn to hide it from others and themselves.

My purpose for including the generational perspective is that I have consistently observed shame and self-blame in perfectionists who view themselves as solely responsible and defective as human beings. They carry a heavy burden and are very reluctant to share that blame with their parents or anyone else. I am suggesting here that we give up blaming entirely and consider the struggles of those around you from a much broader perspective. To illustrate, I would like to share a story with you of three generations who did the best that they could with what they had.

A TALE OF THREE FAMILIES

Once upon a time, two young couples—I will call them the Joneses, who resided in a small town in Northern Virginia and the O'Briens, who lived in the borough of Brooklyn in New York—lived under sharply contrasting moral, social, and economic standards; and they had nothing in common, or so they believed.

The Joneses

The Joneses were a couple everyone admired. Jeff Jones was the pastor of the largest church in their community. He was a handsome, well-dressed, upstanding man who worked long hours without complaint, serving both his congregation and the town through active involvement on boards and in citizens' groups. He was doing the same job his father had done, in the same community. It felt right for him from a very early age.

On a personal level, Jeff was very controlled—a perfectionist, for sure, and proud of it. He knew the right way to do almost anything, from driving a car to living in general. He never lost his temper and was perceived as a man who could support others through a crisis but would never have one himself. When he was angry or upset, he would deny it, and if anyone happened to witness him having a bad moment, Jeff felt ashamed and weak. He hated vulnerability and losing control, in both himself and anyone else. He used his work to avoid this discomfort by staying focused and relying on the structure and responsibilities of his life.

Jeff had very strong opinions about how others should live and behave. In private, particularly at home, he did not hesitate to criticize and control his family. After a few glasses of wine, he would loosen up and speak more freely, with a tone of sarcasm but always about the deficiencies of others, including his wife, Joann. Jeff really had two lives: a public one, in which he was upbeat, friendly, and compassionate (his coworkers called this his "telephone voice"), and a private one, in which he was moody and withdrawn.

Joann Jones was an attractive woman with a pleasant smile, outside the home. She was very conscious of the image she was projecting to others and didn't want to offend anyone or make a social error. She was afraid of Jeff's temper, seething just under the surface, when he disapproved of the way she did things. She was careful to check herself to prevent that from happening. Joann had a part-time job that did not interfere with her household, social, and church responsibilities.

In their home, Joann was very busy with a list of duties. She did not choose to do them; they were expected of her. She secretly resented the backseat she took to her husband but never let on that it bothered her. After all, she chose to support and make life easier for him. She enjoyed the attention they received from the congregation and the status of being the pastor's wife. However, sometimes when he was preaching, she secretly thought, *If they only knew him, they wouldn't admire him so much.* If her anger started surfacing, Joann just said she was stressed and got a prescription from the doctor to calm herself.

The community saw the Joneses as a perfect couple, though perhaps a little stiff. They never argued, but they never really had alone time together, either. They were always with other couples or families. Among friends, they might tease a little and poke sarcastically at each other's faults, but they never had a fight.

The unspoken standards that guided the Joneses were not terribly spiritual, despite their church involvement. They were as follows:

- You are what you do.
- Logic and reason are better than emotions.
- If you look good, you *are* good.
- You must serve as a role model for others.
- Don't let others see your problems.
- Do the right thing.

After three years of marriage, the Joneses eventually had a son. He was their only child; they named him Jeffrey Jr. Little Jeffrey was a jovial, curious child who was interested in everything. He loved sports and drawing, especially on the walls when he was little, but he received quick disapproval for that and any other "inappropriate" behavior. Jeffrey had to learn to control his urges, or he would be scolded and rejected by his mother. Sometimes, when Mom was particularly upset with Dad, she would be very critical of Jeffrey Jr.

He saw very little of Dad, but as he was growing up, people often told Jeffrey what a good man his father was and how lucky he was to be in this family. From Jeffrey's point of view, Mom did not seem to be very fond of Dad, although she never really said that.

Jeffrey was a good student and athlete. He had a few friends who were carefully screened by Mom for their acceptability. People thought of him as a good person, intelligent, and active. Jeffrey had a few disappointments in his life. He was not allowed to play football, although he was very good at it, and he was pressured into an accelerated academic program, even though he didn't feel as smart as the other kids in it. When he told his parents how he felt, they told him not to feel that way and that they knew best. After a while, he stopped having those feelings and just complied with their expectations. If he wanted to act out, he did it away from the family and the church. He was good at hiding, and he felt dishonest and a bit like an impostor when his parents boasted about how good and easy he was.

Sometimes Jeffrey would try especially hard at something with the hope that his father would notice and give him some attention. Mostly, however, Dad found fault and continued to push. Overall, Jeffrey had anything he needed and felt very prepared for life. If anyone asked, he said (and believed), "Everything is great!"

The O'Briens

The O'Briens had a very different sort of home. They lived in a lower-middle-class neighborhood in Brooklyn. Jerry O'Brien was a laborer who had difficulty finding and keeping work because of his bad back and his drinking. When he was sober, Jerry was quiet and a bit depressed. When he drank, he rarely came home. When he was at home, he was angry and, in later years, sometimes violent.

Jerry was an avid bowler. All of his friends bowled, and they spent many nights each week at the bowling alley. He almost never came home when he was expected. He spent money on beer, bowling, and betting on games. The family was suffering because of this. Jerry and his wife, Maureen, had terrible fights about Jerry's bowling and his friends. The fights were loud, and sometimes the neighbors would call the police.

Jerry appeared to be totally self-centered and insensitive to those around him. He frequently blamed his wife for his absences and his drinking. He threatened to leave, saying she could not survive without him, but he never did.

Maureen O'Brien had hoped to be taken care of by the wonderful man she had first known. When they met, he was a bit wild but also kind and loving. Time had taken its toll, however, and it seemed that Jerry would never change. Both Jerry and Maureen came from alcoholic families. They didn't expect much from life. To Maureen, happiness would have been having a husband who would never hit her and who brought a paycheck home.

Maureen was a nurse's aide in a nursing home, taking care of sick and elderly patients on the night shift. She was preoccupied while she was at work with the thought that something terrible would happen at home. For a while, she called home frequently but would only end up fighting with Jerry on the phone. Over time, she began to lose hope, and she hardened in her anger. She just didn't care anymore. Having a husband—even one like Jerry—was better than being alone.

When she was younger, Maureen had left Jerry a few times. But he would promise to change, so she had always come back for the sake of the children. At home and around her own family, Maureen complained endlessly about Jerry. She truly believed that if only he would change, she would be fine. Maureen used food for comfort and became obese over the years. She did not care about her appearance or about the house. She slept as much as she could, because she didn't have to feel when she was asleep.

Jerry and Maureen had three children: Kate, Todd, and Linda, all two years apart. When Kate was born, Jerry and Maureen were unprepared, since they had only been dating a few months when Maureen got pregnant. Maureen hoped that the baby would help to settle Jerry down, keeping him home more often. Kate was a pleasant child: smiling, cooperative, and quiet. She didn't demand much and was seen as independent and capable.

As Jerry's drinking increased, the arguments often centered on his feeling pressured because Maureen insisted on having children and was always too tired to have sex or keep him company. Kate heard the arguments, and in her mind they meant that he went out and drank because of her. At a very early age, Kate began to take care of her mother.

Often, after an argument, even when Kate was only three or four, Maureen sat in the kitchen crying and depressed. Kate brushed her mother's hair and told her it would be okay, that "Daddy will be home soon." Maureen would be grateful for the support and say, "I don't know what I'd do without you." For that brief moment, Kate felt important and not alone. She learned that if you take care of others and are very good, sometimes they will give you something back.

She also learned that if she fixed the problems when she was scared, she wasn't scared anymore. As she grew up, Kate became aware that other children did not have homes like hers. She, her brother, and her sister lay in bed terrified of the sounds downstairs, not daring to say a word, even to one another. She began to dream of the day when she would leave home and create the kind of family she saw on television and at her friends' houses.

Kate was an excellent student. She was often chosen for special tasks in the classroom, she tutored other children, and she was active in almost anything she could find. When she came home, Kate cleaned the house, cooked, and took care of her brother and her sister. She discovered that the busier she was, the less depressed and worried she felt. As long as she didn't make any mistakes, she was fine. In fact, she received much praise outside her home. She never believed it, since she knew who she really was and they didn't. If she failed at something, said the wrong thing, or disappointed someone, she was devastated and ashamed. She would avoid people, work harder, and focus on other people's problems.

Kate held on to the belief that someday she would do it differently—the "right" way. Kate dreamed about being a doctor but decided to become a teacher and to have a perfect family of her own.

Her siblings, Todd and Linda, adapted to the situation, too, each in his or her own way. Todd could not compete with his older sister and got more attention from being the family problem child. Todd struggled with anything he did. He fought with other children in nursery school and continued this pattern throughout his school years. The more stressful things were at home, the more he would act out. Ironically, Todd felt rejected but pushed people away and blamed them for not wanting him. He was afraid much of the time and had to hide it. He thought that he should have been the man in the house, but he never felt capable. He wanted to protect his mother and make her proud, but he failed.

Todd discovered marijuana when he was fourteen, which made him feel as good as his peers. It was easy to blame his father for that. Kate did everything she could to stop him from smoking, but he strongly resented her meddling and did not want another parent. Todd's parents found him to be a distraction from their arguments and at times focused on him as the primary problem in the home. Both parents thought that they had failed with Todd.

The youngest, Linda, became invisible. She found safety in her isolation and felt better when she didn't know what was going on. Linda was an introvert, spending most of her time in her room, eating while she watched television or reading. She didn't bother anyone and remained average and unnoticed throughout her childhood. Kate felt responsible for her little sister but did not know how to help her.

Kate and Jeffrey Meet

Two attractive, intelligent people met on a blind date when they were sophomores in college. Kate O'Brien was studying English on a scholarship, planning to be a high school English teacher. She had always known exactly what she was looking for in a future mate: the opposite of Dad—responsible, secure, a light drinker, hardworking, and emotionally stable. Jeffrey Jones was just starting to consider law school and had a bright future ahead of him. Although he was a good conversationalist, Kate had a hard time figuring him out. She found this confusing but decided that in time he would open up and share himself with her. She especially liked his family—it looked so normal and healthy. He was exactly what she wanted. She felt lucky that he wanted her.

Jeffrey hadn't given much thought to the idea of marriage or what he wanted in a wife (except that she should fit in with his lifestyle), but he was immediately attracted to Kate. He felt a little sorry for her, with her messed-up family, but he also liked the challenge of it. Jeffrey's parents were not particularly pleased with his choice, and for once that felt good, too.

Kate looked great and knew how to fit in, and when Jeffrey was with her, he felt like a better man. She had goals and was independent. She also gave him good advice about his own future. After graduation, Kate started to talk about marriage and children, and he went along even though he wasn't sure he was ready. Jeffrey was busy planning his career.

Once they were married, they just knew things would work out. Kate was determined enough for both of them. She got a job as a teacher, working full-time and also working on an online graduate degree. Jeffrey took a low-paying job in a law practice. Together they created the perfect home, and they looked like a perfect couple on their way into a great future.

Without ever having a conversation about it, they had made a silent pact about four very important things:

1. "The past is the past—I won't ask you about your childhood if you don't ask me about mine."

2. "I'll do what's expected of me, but don't expect me to be vulnerable."
3. Kate will be happy as long as Jeffrey goes along with her plan.
4. Jeffrey will be happy as long as there is peace.

They ran into a few difficulties early in their relationship, but it was nothing they couldn't overlook. Kate tended to overreact to small things—at least that's what Jeffrey said. Actually, she would hold her feelings in as long as she could and then blow up.

Their discussions (not arguments, since "good" couples don't argue) about Jeffrey's lack of communication and affection would often result in Kate getting hysterical while Jeffrey became increasingly rational and distant. Since Jeffrey was not in touch with his feelings, he didn't know what she was talking about. To her frequent question of "Well, do you love me?" he would respond, "Of course I do. I married you, didn't I?"

Jeffrey never felt the actual feeling of love, but he had some idea of what he was supposed to do. Every once in a while he would kiss her for no reason or bring her flowers. Kate would then ask, "What do you want now?" They both knew this wasn't exactly what they expected from marriage, but it was okay. What they needed was a distraction from each other.

Children would be the perfect distraction, Kate thought. She felt very competent in this area. Jeffrey wasn't as sure about having kids, but Kate seemed to be good at everything, so why not? Kate's vision was that they would share the child-rearing duties and keep both careers as well. She had spent years watching her mother mess up and was determined to be the opposite kind of mom. Whereas her mother had been weak and unreliable, Kate would be strong and always available. Whereas her mother had not been affectionate and didn't talk to her children, Kate would tell her children she loved them every day and communicate with them. Kate wanted what she thought others had and attempted to give it all to her children. She was sure Jeffrey wanted the same things.

Their daughter, Kelly, and their son, Jason, were born three years apart so that she could spend the proper amount of time with each in infancy. She avoided giving her children any unnatural foods and relied on breast-feeding and homemade baby foods. She used only cloth diapers because she had always been very concerned about the environment. Kate believed it was very important to read to her children every day and felt guilty when she wasn't able to do this. Jeffrey tried to keep up, but he felt inept, since he had been an only child, and preferred to do tasks at which he felt competent. Work was the best place to do that, and he was well liked and appreciated there.

Kelly and Jason took piano lessons and also played soccer. Jason was talented and on several teams, which took up much of the family's time. They were a very busy family, out almost every night with some activity. Kate was active in the PTA and eventually became president for a few years.

Kate's mother called her daily for continued moral support and to subtly remind her that she had abandoned them. Kate's brother, Todd, was in more serious trouble these days and needed some financial help, and Linda had recently moved away. Kate continued to feel responsible and guilty for leaving, but she tried to keep those family problems away from her children. Kelly and Jason did not know that their grandfather was an alcoholic, and they would never find out from Kate.

Jeffrey's family came over every Sunday for dinner. They expressed their hostility to Kate indirectly through sarcasm, remarks about her housekeeping, questions about her father, and other sensitive subjects. When Kate would ask Jeffrey to intervene for her, he acted as though he didn't notice anything. The Joneses were actually wonderful with Kelly and Jason, which made Kate feel even more inadequate, since she didn't allow her parents to see her children.

Jeffrey's career really began to take off. Kate blamed his work for the deterioration of their marriage, but she clung to the hope that relief was over the next hill. When Jeffrey had a brief affair, Kate forgave him and buried herself in the intensity of her job and the children's activities. She blamed herself for the affair. She was preoccupied with her parents but felt helpless to do anything other than rescue them and lecture them when a crisis arose. Any time spent away from her children caused her to feel guilty. She wasn't doing enough for her marriage and needed to try harder.

Although Jason and Kelly were always well dressed and polite in accordance with Kate's childhood dreams, they were definitely not perfect. Underneath the facade of the perfect family, Jason had a learning disability, which kept Kate busy visiting the school, taking him to tutoring, and working with him at home on his reading. She took it personally when Jason struggled, and he began to hide his problems from her because of her overreaction and hovering.

Kelly was a little overweight, which was very disturbing to Kate. Kelly seemed like a happy child, but Kate continued to worry and controlled Kelly's diet and appearance. Kate felt inadequate and guilty as a mother. Kelly began to feel the pressure of her mother's guilt and felt responsible for it. Kelly believed that she was the problem. Her parents, especially her mom, were doing everything for her, and she was not good enough. She was depressed and began bingeing and purging, which helped her to feel better about herself.

Jason and Kelly had always been told that they were very lucky children. Every day they were told that they were loved, and they had everything they could want. When they had a problem, they got a great deal of attention; but their mother was very busy most of the time (doing the right things) and did not really talk to them about their feelings. Dad was absent, working hard to take care of them, and was like a moving target when they approached him. He would listen for a minute, provide an answer to their problems, and move on. He was the same way with Kate. They were barely speaking.

Kate became increasingly stressed with her chaotic life. Since she had been a little girl, her pattern was to keep moving forward, one decision or one chore at a time. She tried not to notice how she felt, but it was becoming more difficult each day. If only she could get it all done and be certain that her parents and her children were okay, she could relax and breathe. If only Jeffrey would help out more, it might work out. She had been chasing that dream every day of her life.

Jeffrey's pattern was to stay out of any possible conflict or confrontation, which he did by being a nice guy who was liked by everyone except his wife. He couldn't understand what she wanted from him and was tired of being criticized. His passivity and refusal to fully commit to the relationship created an impasse.

We never know when the day will come that the mountain is just too big to climb for one more minute—until it happens. Kate taught advanced placement English at her children's school, and one Monday morning she was informed by a peer that her son, currently in middle school, was going to be held back a grade and would not be moving on to high school. Kate knew that his immaturity and learning disability would make it harder for him as a freshman, but she felt embarrassed and hurt. She tried to reach Jeffrey, but he was not available and didn't respond to her message. She had to forget about it for now.

Later the same day, she got a phone call from her mother, who was crying after being threatened by her father. Kate could not let any of this interfere with her work, so she just put it in the back of her mind and told no one how upset she was. She would deal with it all later. In her last-period class, one of her more challenging students came to class high. Kate lost it. She confronted him in front of the class. "Don't you know what you're doing to yourself and your family?" she yelled. She then dismissed him from the class. Her students and coworkers were shocked. Kate had never lost control before. She was devastated and ashamed.

She was advised by the principal to take a few days off and to seek counseling. Kate was distraught and knew it was time to do something about her situation. She began to see the unmanageability in her life and her family. She began weekly counseling and took a leave of absence. In time, Kate began to realize that she had become her mother, putting up with a failing marriage, being out of touch with her children's feelings, and dying on the inside. She saw the futility of trying to overcome the past by being perfect. Kate came to the realization that she (like her mother) had done the very best she knew how, giving everything she had while neglecting herself and her marriage. It was time to face it all and to admit that she could not overcome the painful legacy of her family on her own, and as time passed, she could see that it was no one's fault.

Jason and Kelly would never have described their family as abusive or even as dysfunctional, yet they were living with the residual, painful dynamics of their parents and their grandparents on both sides of the family. Perfectionists like Kate will try to overcome huge emotional struggles by simply doing the right thing. No amount of effort could have insulated Jason or Kelly from the effects of what happened in their parents' past. When Kate's work crisis occurred, Kelly believed that her weight had become an issue that troubled her mother and Jason knew that his parents were very disappointed in his academic problems.

In "looking-good" families, where there is no visible problem such as parents arguing, addiction or mental illness to explain the anxiety they feel, children tend to blame themselves. They think that they have failed their parents. Some children will try harder to help their parents and some may rebel and distance themselves from the family. History was repeating itself and could only be turned around if someone was willing to face the past and change.

BLOCKS TO HEALTHY RELATIONSHIPS

Do these families seem familiar? Although we all have different stories, we have a great deal in common with other human beings. Whether we resemble the Joneses or the O'Briens, we were all children once with the same need for attachment. For many, those needs are not met or are met inconsistently. Each of the individuals in the story above had a childhood in which needs were unnoticed. Each was raised by parents who were, in a way, starving, needy children. Children who learned to adapt to their surroundings, living on what little love and nurturing was available.

Becoming a perfect child is one way to adapt to a painful family experience. Certainly, Jeffrey's parents, Jeff and Joann, learned that doing what they believed was right gave them some comfort, if not self-worth. Kate and Jeffrey, in their attempt to look good, were hoping to eventually feel good. They had become accustomed to the chaos and lack of connection but found that their focus on external things would not bring them together.

Perfectionism as a compulsive pattern is not present at birth. It develops as a response to stress, which is then positively reinforced by others. Several issues reduce the likelihood of secure attachment existing in children and adults from painful families. Though unknown to the individual, these handicaps become blocks to healthy relationships and are then passed on to the next generation.

Lack of Trust

At birth, we are as perfect as we are supposed to be. There is nothing about us that is unlovable or in need of change, until we encounter parents with a multitude of unresolved problems of their own. Kate was a perfect child who, like all infants, was forced to adapt to the family she was born into. As an infant, Kate knew instinctively that she would not survive unless she had some kind of connection with her mother or her father. She learned through trial and error what it would take to become connected and how to maintain it.

At this time in her fragile life, she was learning about trust. *Will they feed me when I'm hungry, change me when I'm wet, hold me gently when I cry, and smile back at me when I smile? Is this world a safe, predictable, consistent place?* The answer for Kate and many others is no.

When parents' own basic needs for safety, intimacy, and consistency have not been met, they cannot give their children what they did not receive (and thus do not have). When parents are insecure, they still do their best, but without help and guidance, they will not be able to develop a secure parenting style by using only their minds and wills.

Infants and toddlers are capable of learning from their experiences. With continued reinforcement and repetition, they find behaviors that work to get the attention they seek. If they cannot trust their environment the way it is, maybe they can learn to control it. The need to control is always a response to fear. The ultimate fear for both a child and an adult is fear of abandonment, which from the infant's perspective means death. In my work, I frequently meet adults who carry with them irrational fears of being alone. These fears are rooted in very early childhood experiences.

The perfectionist child (described in Chapter 1 as born with a preference for order) in a painful family has discovered that sometimes the better you are, the more love you get. The parents of a perfectionist child, even if they are hurting, will gain some pleasure early in the child's life from his or her achievements. The child is loved for doing, not for being. If the parents are insecure, the hidden message that children get from praise for good behavior or competence is, for example, "You make me feel like a good parent when you walk at ten months! Do more!"

When a child whose emotional needs are not consistently met receives such a wonderful response for doing something well, he or she will do it more often. The excitement of the first steps, smile, or reading, however, cannot sustain a family in pain, and so the validation becomes less frequent. The child learns to wait and survive on crumbs. The pattern is then integrated into other relationships as he or she grows up.

In addition to experiencing inconsistencies in the parents' praise, the child may experience confusion as a result of the parents saying one thing and doing another. Kate, for example, grew up with the dishonesty of an alcoholic family. Jeffrey learned to not trust words, since he often felt internally the anger that was hidden behind the tight smiles of his parents.

The inability to trust leads children to begin their lives in a defensive posture. "I know I'm going to be hurt, so I'd better take care of myself!" For some, perfectionism becomes a very effective way to do this.

Lack of Intimacy and Vulnerability

In the stories above, all members of the three families began with love, but without safety and trust, they were not able to be vulnerable with one another. There are a number of reasons for this difficulty:

1. It is in our nature to reach out to others to give and receive love, but if the result is consistently painful, we give up or settle for less.
2. All of the people in these examples are to some degree shame-based—that is, they feel less than others and fear being abandoned if they reveal themselves fully.
3. When individuals have insecure attachment, they are uncomfortable with potential mates who are open and expect vulnerability. There is a process of natural selection that occurs when two people are at about the same level of emotional security—it just feels better, more like home. This holds true even if we are consciously trying to run away from home and the past.
4. These individuals have been in family systems and communities with others who are not open to vulnerability for so long that they believe that what they are experiencing is normal and do not know what else to look for.

5. People who do not know their own feelings and cannot express them will never be intimate.

Intimacy is an honest emotional connection between two human beings. The intimacy between parent and child will, of course, be very different from that between adult friends or lovers. At least six ingredients are necessary for intimacy to occur:

1. **Self-knowledge.** There must be an *I* to share. We have to know who we are before we can share ourselves with someone else. For example, I am sensitive and I like to talk things through. I love my home and family connections. I wouldn't be me without them. I am not simply the roles I play.
2. **Risk of rejection.** We must be able to face the possibility that with our openness and honesty, rejection is always possible. Intimate relationships are not without conflict. Intimacy comes from sharing good and bad feelings and expressing needs, all without defensiveness. Finding healthy ways to manage the anxiety that comes from separation or rejection is an essential task for all adults who want intimacy.
3. **Shared feelings.** Intimacy is not accomplished by sharing opinions or activities alone. It must include sharing feelings: about life, about me, about you, and about us. Feelings include sadness, fear, anger, guilt, shame, and joy.
4. **Clear boundaries.** These give us a sense of safety. When I know what I need and respect what you need, I do not hold you responsible for my feelings. I do not ask you to be my sole support. I do not need to know everything about you. I don't place excessive demands, nor will I tolerate abuse.
5. **Interdependence.** This suggests a willingness to both give to

and receive from the other. It is the glue that holds a committed relationship together and creates the opportunity for intimacy.

6. **Emotional risk.** Many of us fear intimacy because of the risks involved in getting that close. Clients have often reported, in hindsight, that they have run away from what seemed to be a healthy person because they felt threatened. Sex can be used to avoid intimacy: "You can have my body, as long as I don't have to tell you who I am." It is used as a way to feel something with minimal emotional risk.

Perfectionism may cause a person to appear competent, self-sufficient, and complete. By using it as a defense, the characters in our story—Jeff, Joann, Jeffrey, and Kate—prevented others from reaching out to them. Ironically, in seeking approval so diligently, they actually prevented anyone from filling their needs for love, friendship, support, and connection.

Lack of Identity

Each of us is born with all that we need to discover who we are and how we will best serve our purpose. It begins as potential, visible in our personalities, interests, curiosities, and physical attributes. Then it is mirrored and demonstrated to us by parents, siblings, and the world.

According to my parents, when I was an infant I cried very loudly when I needed something. My movements were described as awkward, attention seeking, energetic, and a little hyper. My interpretation of my parents' description was that I was just "too much." As I have grown to love and accept who I am, I have realized that I was preparing, among other things, to be a public speaker. My work is an expression of all that I am; talking loudly and often is required for what I do. It is an opportunity to use my gifts for my own pleasure and to make a contribution to others. It would have been great to know that earlier in life.

To be effective as parents, we need to allow our children to just be what they are, providing guidance and safety while they evolve into their full potential. It can be complicated for a parent who has traits similar to his or her child and who needs to provide support that he or she did not receive for those traits.

A common example might be a boy who is sensitive and doesn't have an interest in sports. He needs guidance to find his interests and possibly deal with the emotions that go with not fitting in. If a dad had the same traits and was shamed as a child, he might need to seek help to guide his son.

Jeffrey, the son of two rigid, repressed perfectionists, did not have a chance to find out who he was. In order to be connected to and accepted by his parents, he had to be what they expected. Very early in his life, he began to give up parts of himself. As an adult, even though he was very successful and well liked, he never felt any satisfaction with his work or his relationships. He had developed a pseudo-self—in a sense, he was having an out-of-body experience. He was unable to look inside and reflect on the question, "Is this who I really want to be?" Vulnerability was seen as weakness in his family, and to strengthen his marriage by being intimate and guiding his children, he would need to learn to be present and authentic.

Children who live in painful families are not asked who they are. Parents believe they are responsible for raising their children to be good people who get jobs, form relationships, and fit in. Jeffrey was not asked, "Who are you? What do you like to eat? Would you rather play football or piano?" He complied with the rules, got a minimum of approval, and lost himself in the process.

It is sad that children such as Jeffrey and Kate, and their own children, do what they have to do to survive with the least amount of pain necessary. By the time they reach the crisis that drives them to examine themselves (this may be a midlife crisis, an empty nest, a severe depression, or the end of a relationship), they have no sense of who they are, and they will need professional help to begin the search for the authentic self that was lost.

Perfectionism can be a substitute, though an ineffective one, for identity. We may begin to define ourselves by the roles we play and judge ourselves based on how perfectly we play them. The greater the need to be perfect, the weaker the identity of the person within.

Shame

Shame is perhaps the single greatest factor contributing to perfectionism. When a child feels flawed and responsible for the family's problems, as Kate did, she needs to compensate for the sense of worthlessness. She believed that she was not loved because she wasn't good enough. In painful families, children have three basic choices in response to the stress:

1. **Compliance with what they believe is expected of them.** This is frequently the choice of the firstborn, but only if that approach fits the child's personality. He or she will find out what the rules are (even if they keep changing) and try to follow them. The complier who gets occasional positive results will probably develop this as a lifetime pattern. Born leaders are prone to this pattern, as are those with an

abundance of compassion for and sensitivity to others.

2. **Resistance to anything that appears to be rigid or authoritarian.** There are many forms of resistance, some quiet and thoughtful, some outward and defiant. If the firstborn has opted for compliance, the second child, like Todd in our story, may find resistance to be more effective if he has what I like to call a feisty temperament. This is the child who always asks why, says no, and challenges the status quo. He may be intelligent, verbal, and a maverick. Kids will do whatever it takes to be noticed. If negative behavior gets the focus of the family, they may use it.
3. **Becoming invisible as another way to survive.** The invisible child, like Linda in our story, will find safety within herself. She will develop an ability to go inside to a safe place and actually tune out the stress. If she is an introvert, she may be skilled at not being noticed: wearing drab colors, speaking quietly, avoiding eye contact, and being average in every way. Most of us will recall a period in our lives when we withdrew; some have done it for a lifetime. If she is an extrovert, she may surround herself with peers and blend in. She may avoid closeness and prefer to stay out of the house as much as possible. She is then alone even in a crowd. (See the avoidant attachment style in Chapter 2.)

In our culture, it is assumed that a compliant, achieving, good child has high self-worth; however, all three of these roles represent children, and later adults, who are shame-based, which correlates with low self-esteem. They have found ways to cover their inadequacies and to protect themselves with an armor of compulsive behavior.

Overt perfectionists rarely make mistakes but struggle internally with the knowledge that if they show a flaw, they will be seen as worthless and rejected. A great example in the story above was Kate's outburst toward a student in front of the class. Thoughts like *What will others think of me? How could I have done that?*,and *I am bad* are continually buzzing in the mind of the perfectionist. This feeling is sometimes called guilt, but, in reality, it is shame. Guilt is a response to having made a mistake. Shame is a feeling, deep within, of actually *being* a mistake. Guilt is short-lived; shame stays with us for a long time, and it is often medicated with chemicals or compulsive behavior. Kate suffered months of shame and remorse after what she did. Someone less "perfect" may have felt a bit guilty or embarrassed but would have been over it in days. The fact that it was public compounded it.

Summary

In this chapter we took an inside view of three family systems that appeared to be very different. Looking inside these families at their emotional experiences and their attachments made it possible to see them primarily as human beings who want to love and be loved. They were obviously lost, were unable to navigate their relationships in a healthy way, and may have been without a single role model for several generations.

Kate and Jeffrey had what it would take intellectually, but they could not create the emotional foundation for a healthy relationship or family life. There is no one to blame for their problems, and no easy fix would be able to turn this around. Without some type of serious intervention, nothing will change.

We examined some of the most significant blocks to healthy relationships, the things that keep good people from achieving what they set out to do. The issues of trust, intimacy, identity, and shame are challenges for perfectionists and for anyone from a painful family. The good news is that it is never too late to begin the process of change. We are capable of growing in each of these areas, and it can make a huge difference across generations when one person finds the courage to face the past and change the future.

Chapter 6

Learning to Live in the Middle

The decision to become more human—that is, less perfect—is not an easy one to make, despite the fact that we know we have been trying to accomplish the impossible. Before you make a commitment to this change, I'd like to suggest a brief exercise.

THE PITFALLS AND BENEFITS OF PERFECTIONISM

You are going to make two lists, as described below. My personal lists are provided as a guide. First do the following:

1. Write a list of all of the benefits your perfectionism provides.
2. Write a list of all of the pitfalls of your perfectionism: what you don't like about it or what it takes from your life.
3. Rate each benefit according to its overall importance or value in your life on a scale of 1 to 5 (1 = little value, 5 = very valuable).
4. Rate each pitfall according to how much it bothers you or detracts from your life (1 = doesn't really bother me, 5 = bothers me a great deal).

When you are finished, count how many items are listed in each section. As you can see below, my list has seven benefits and eight pitfalls. Then total the points for benefits and the points for pitfalls. I have 20 points for benefits and 36 for pitfalls.

The Benefits of Being a Perfectionist

1. I get to feel superior at times 1
2. I accomplish a great deal in a little time 4
3. People look up to me for support and help 3
4. I have succeeded professionally using this method 4
5. My life is often orderly, structured, and sensible 4
6. I have a fleeting sense of control over my life 2
7. I get strokes for looking superhuman 2

Total: 20 points

The Pitfalls of Being a Perfectionist

1. I can be very isolated when I am being perfect 5
2. I don't have enough quiet time because I'm always *doing* 4
3. I am in the role of leader more than I like 3
4. My parenting becomes rigid and critical when I try to be perfect 5
5. I suffer from the physical effects of the stress I impose on myself 5
6. If I look like I am superwoman, then that's what others expect of me 5
7. I take on responsibility that isn't mine, believing others can't do it as well 4
8. It isn't fun 5

Total: 36 points

DECIDING TO CHANGE

You may find that the number of benefits is greater than the number of pitfalls, but when you look at the total number of points, you may discover that the benefits actually have less value or significance in your life. Our reasons for hanging on to this compulsion don't make much sense when we compare them to things we care about, like intimacy, peace of mind, joy, or good parenting. Ask yourself if it is worth it to keep trying to be perfect.

You make the decision to give up your perfectionism one day, even one moment, at a time. Imperfection is something you may not be able to adhere to consistently but can view as an overall goal. Since personal growth is not an intellectual process, the choice to let go of control is a very important first step. You will make it many times over in the days and years ahead.

Whenever I speak before an audience on the subject of perfectionism, people inevitably have questions about their spouses, children, and friends who have the characteristics I am discussing. They want very much for the other person to change, often out of love but also for selfish reasons. Living with a perfectionist or any compulsive person is not easy. Others generally see our problem long before we do.

Unfortunately, the frustration of others is rarely strong enough motivation for a perfectionist to begin the long, uncomfortable process of change. You will probably not be able to sustain the effort for someone else.

I do not believe that being a perfectionist automatically means that one needs counseling. If our lives have become unmanageable, as described in Chapter 4, and we want very much to have different lives, counseling may be helpful and can accelerate the process. If we are in denial about the severity and have not noticed the harm it is causing to those we love, we may need their help to lovingly point this out to us. When that happens, we may be able to feel a personal need to change and begin the process. The most striking motivations in my experience with clients are (1) the desire to be a better parent, and (2) the desire to save a relationship.

It may be hard to admit, but when we try to diagnose others (with the exception of those in severe physical or emotional crises), it is usually our *own* compulsive behavior that we are struggling with.

If you are on the fence about whether this issue is important for you, ask three people who care about you if they think your perfectionism is a problem. If they agree that it is, pay attention to this old saying, often used in twelve-step programs: "If it walks like a duck and talks like a duck, it's a duck." If everyone thinks you're a duck, you probably are. Try surrendering, and take it one step at a time.

CHANGING FROM THE INSIDE OUT

Many perfectionists have spent their lives trying to look okay. This presents a problem when they finally decide to get help. Suzanne, a former client, described herself as a perfectionist and a compulsive caretaker. She was great at focusing on the needs of others and generally assumed the role of the strong one in her relationships. Although she had many friends, most of them were very dependent and rarely asked her how she was. They assumed that she couldn't possibly have any problems, since she looked so well put together and never asked for anything.

Occasionally, when Suzanne had a bad day and needed some support, she would call a friend and ask, "How are you?" hoping in vain that during the course of the conversation the friend would notice the depressed tone in her voice. The conversation would inevitably turn into the friend giving Suzanne an update on her own issues, but since the friend never asked how Suzanne was, the conversation never got around to meeting her needs.

The next day, still feeling low, she would go to work, dressing as nicely as ever, and bury herself in her job. She might actually find work to be a good distraction and perform a little better than usual. At lunch a longtime coworker might ask, "Are you okay? You're a little quiet today." Suzanne would answer, "Oh, I'm fine, just a little overwhelmed with work." The conversation quickly returned to the needs of her coworker.

Suzanne has been trying for years to get love and approval from others by being good and taking care of them. She has hoped that they would reciprocate out of gratitude. They believe that she is fine because that is how she looks and what she says. Ironically, the things she fears the most—abandonment and isolation from others—are exactly what her behavior is bringing about.

Many of the efforts people use to overcome shame, such as perfectionism and caretaking, create the impression that these people do not need anything. Their "goodness" puts them at a distance, since others feel inadequate in comparison.

I often visualize this as the perfectionist unconsciously standing on a pedestal or a chair above other people—not because they feel superior but because they needed to be able to be aware of and see everything around them. They also don't want to be so close to others that they would be vulnerable. The chair puts the perfectionist at ease and in control. Those who are standing around the chair see the perfectionist as capable of anything, including solving their problems and carrying a larger share of responsibility.

I remember that when I made the choice to change and let go, it meant stepping down off the chair and exposing my true self. It felt like jumping into ice water, suddenly becoming real and vulnerable. It is scary to ask for help, to say no, and to let people know you. It also triggers shame that somehow now you are nobody, you don't know your purpose, and you don't know how to connect with those around you. I felt all of those things.

At first, your friends and your family will not acknowledge your needs or your pain, and they may even insist that you're fine because you appear to be. Personal growth requires changing your insides so that they match up with your outsides. This means looking sad when you are sad, getting tired when you have worked hard, needing support, and being vulnerable. It cannot be accomplished by simply reading books or studying the behavior of others (that was one of my personal favorites).

This chapter provides a general road map for change in three stages. Because I know what perfectionists are like, I have to emphasize that it is okay to zigzag to your goal, take detours, or find another way that works for you. This is not the only way, and it isn't a mandate.

STAGE 1: IDENTIFYING THE PROBLEM

The act of reading this book is an attempt to identify or name the difficulties you may be experiencing in your life. Giving the problem a name is useful at this stage and brings some relief from the guilt and shame of struggling alone. You did not get this way all by yourself. You are part of a family and a world that helped you along. You have a particular compulsive pattern of behavior that served you well, but it no longer makes sense.

Many others have the same problem, and we can even laugh at the absurdity of trying to be perfect. You are not alone. This is good news!

You will learn many important things during the identification stage. Much of this you can get on your own from reading and talking and listening to others, perhaps at self help meetings or in a therapy group. Anyone who wants to "get off the chair" will benefit from reaching out for support and taking a giant leap forward by beginning to share with others.

Coming out as an imperfect human being can increase shame temporarily, yet it is also the antidote for shame. Shame will never be healed if you do not have people who care about you and are willing to be a mirror or an advocate for what you are doing. Relying only on the voice in your head is not much help when it comes to shame.

Because you are open, you will find some things you are glad to discover and others you'd rather not know. This is all part of the process. Here are some examples:

- You realize that your children have been hurt by what you thought was excellent parenting.
- You find that the family you were raised in was a painful or stressful one. In some cases, it may have been abusive.
- You remember painful events in your adult relationships and see that they are much like what you saw between your parents as a child.
- You discover that you are a very critical and/or controlling person and feel ashamed of it. You will need to balance that with the knowledge that your fears were driving that behavior.
- You find that you have new choices since you've learned that you can change your pattern if you're willing to work at it.
- You talk to old friends and find that while some of them don't

want you to be imperfect, others have wanted to reach out to you but didn't know how to help you "off the chair."

- You learn or are reminded of simple but important concepts such as these: Feelings aren't bad or good. Fighting your feelings or pushing them away just makes things worse. It helps to talk. Your needs are as important as the needs of others (including children), and it is your job to make yourself happy.

Memories may start to surface, but they often bring a great deal of confusion. Everything you once thought you understood has been reframed to look like something else. Perfectionism felt like an asset; now it's a defect. You don't know if you can trust your own perceptions anymore. You don't know who your friends are. You may trust that the new things you are hearing from your new support system feel right inside, and you may temporarily become dependent on others for a reality check.

Painful feelings will begin to surface with the realization of difficulties or abuse you experienced in the past. The immediate temptation is to avoid the pain by denying, minimizing, forgetting, or even focusing more on what you have done to others, especially your children. It is necessary to begin with what happened to you. This requires a short visit to a painful past, not something to be dwelled upon while blaming and wallowing for months or years. The goal is to feel it now and move through it.

The ultimate goal is to improve your quality of life. If your childhood history is part of that process, it will be important to pause there. The most valuable information to be gained is about your own temperament and how you may have coped with attachment injuries and the anxiety of feeling disconnected from your parents. Remember that the common denominator in all of your problems is you—not your story, but *you.*

Many adults who come from painful families are unaware of what happened in the past that resulted in feelings of insecurity. There are differences from one family to the next in what would be considered harmful to children. Those who have suffered from severe abuse tend to believe that anything other than physical or sexual abuse is normal and acceptable. They don't understand that even without the extreme abuses, they may have suffered psychologically and emotionally. This is important because they need to know that there is more to healthy relationships than the absence of abuse.

Adults raised in looking-good families have received good physical care but may have been emotionally neglected or shamed. I define as injurious or harmful any actions that intentionally or unintentionally damage the self-esteem of a child. Some of the lesser-known injuries that are faced in the identification stage are emotional neglect, shame as discipline, praise without affirmation, violation of boundaries, and repression of feelings.

Emotional Neglect

Chapter 2 dealt with attachment needs in early childhood and the importance of secure attachment. *Emotional neglect* is another way of describing inconsistent attachment. When parents have secure attachment styles, they are able to easily recognize and respond with nurturing and comfort when a child is upset or needs something, even if the child is not able to express it verbally.

When parents have developed an insecure attachment style that is anxious, avoidant, or fearful-avoidant (see Chapter 2 for descriptions of these), they cannot override their established pattern just because they love their children. Parents will struggle with closeness, empathy, touch, and attention with their children and in their adult intimate relationships. From a child's perspective, this means that he or she is seen and cared for when a need is obvious or when others might be watching, but the parent is easily distracted or inattentive when their own needs are unmet.

One of the most damaging aspects of emotional neglect is the absence of reassurance of a child by the parent. One client named Derek gave a good example in group therapy. He was a feisty, or spirited, child who at age five would do things that were contrary to the rules of his parents. He took things from his baby brother and made him cry, he sometimes didn't eat his vegetables, he occasionally spilled his milk, and he got dirty (and required cleaning up) just when they were about to go out. Meanwhile, his parents were going through a hard time. As an adult, he recalled that there was talk about another woman, so his father may have had an affair. His parents were arguing a lot at that time, sometimes during the day and sometimes when he was in bed at night but not asleep.

A five-year-old is not capable of understanding the nature of adult relationships. He only knows that the two most important people in his life are not happy—and not very happy with him. Derek assumed, as is natural for children, that his behavior was the problem. He worried that his parents would get divorced and that he would be alone.

Derek's parents did not realize how he felt or what he was thinking. They also didn't know that it was very important to tell him that it wasn't his fault and that he was loved. Their approach might have included an apology for scaring him by fighting in front of him and an opportunity for him to ask questions. Without reassurance, Derek need) their children to be well behaved, successful in school and career, good-looking, competent, and kind in order to validate the parents' worth or to overcome their painful pasts. Unfortunately, the motivation of the parents may at times be to make themselves feel good as parents rather than to give the children opportunities to feel good about themselves. Self-worth does not come from the outside. Praise is attached to doing things that please the parents.

In an effort to be a good parent, Mom or Dad may give praise and rewards for doing, accomplishing, and succeeding but may neglect to affirm and validate the worth of the child's essence. The only way to get more praise is to do more. Many children learn to wait a very long time from one moment of praise to the next—perhaps years. However well-intentioned the parents may be, it is necessary for children to learn to feel okay when they do nothing as well as when they achieve.

In order to find balance, affirmation must be present on a daily basis. My guess is that you might not have received affirmations from our parents like the following:

- "When you were born, I was so happy."
- "I'm lucky to have a child like you."
- "I love you no matter what."
- "I love all parts of you: your humor, the way you laugh, how nice you are to your friends."
- "I want you to be yourself."
- "It's okay to try new things and take risks."
- I believe in you."

rming through action is as simple as saying hi, making eye , touching the head, smiling, remembering things that are nt to your children, giving full attention, noticing their natu-

silently held the belief throughout his life that he was a big problem for his parents and that he hurt people without even knowing why.

Other signs of emotional neglect are the absence of touch, eye contact, and one-to-one verbal communication as well as ignoring or dismissing the emotions of a child. Our expectations of adult relationships are based on the attachment experiences we have had in childhood. The patterns we develop (e.g., perfectionism) become more compulsive as our internal pain increases.

Shame as Discipline

It is hard to believe that there are still people who use physical punishment to discipline their children. Hitting children, who count on their parents to protect them and guide them, is obviously harmful. They may not be hurt bodily, but their ability to trust is damaged, and they do not learn to manage their own actions through natural or logical consequences.

In recent years, it has been fairly well established that physical punishment does not work. This means that parents who did not have a good alternative had to find another way to control their children's behavior. Punishment of any kind is actually the least effective method, because it doesn't teach anything about what happened, except that a parent will impose penalties or deprive the children of something significant if they misbehave. Fear of the parent's disapproval and losing a privilege is certainly better than hitting, but it isn't as effective as natural and logical consequences provided in a loving way.

Natural consequences are not imposed by a parent but are experienced by the child as a natural result of their behavior or choices (e.g., not studying leads to a failing grade). If a natural consequence would be harmful or ineffective, a parent may design and impose logical consequences. For example, if a four-year-old runs into the street without looking, it is an issue of readiness or immaturity, not bad behavior. A parent may gently remove the child from the situation and take precautions to prevent that from happening again, rather than spanking or punishing. At the same time, a parent will let the child know the dangers of running into the street and explain that someday soon they will be ready to play outside with friends, but they aren't ready for that today. This approach is an example of using a logical consequence because the natural consequence of letting the child be hit by a car is not acceptable.

When parents who were raised in shame-based families decide against spanking their children, the only tools they have available to them are rejection (withdrawal of love) and shame (expressed verbally).

As children, perfectionists may have heard such statements as the following:

- "You'll never be good enough."
- "Why can't you be like your brother [or sister]?"
- "Is that the best you can do?"
- "Why didn't you get an A?"
- "Sit up straight, dress right, talk right, be what I want you to be."
- "What will people think?"
- "I'm so disappointed in you."
- "I thought you were better than that."
- "No one will want to be your friend."

Adults in therapy often report having been called names: *worthless, whore, slut, loser, good-for-nothing,* and worse. The suggestion

that the child is a bad person is contained in each word. Children who make mistakes are not bad; they may have done a bad thing, but they still need love and connection.

Shaming can also occur in a subtler form. Parents or other caregivers, including teachers, may try to control behavior by using nonverbal methods such as a look of disgust, withdrawal, or silence because the child has made a mistake. Another method is to use guilt—"How could you do this to me?"—suggesting that the child is ruining your life or making you sick.

When a parent does not make a mental distinction between t
spirit of a child and the unwanted behavior, children will intern
the belief that they are lovable only if they are perfect. If a parent's
tion to a child is followed by regret and reassurance of the chi
harm is lessened. Without this, a child is left abandoned and co
All parents have bad days where they regret their own reactio
dren can accept that. The perfect child will keep trying to
or at least attention. Some will even punish themselves for

Praise Without Affirmation

Most parents are well acquainted with the impor
praise to children but are less familiar with the valu
According to the dictionary, *praise* may be equat
applause, celebration, or commendation. The
means something a bit different: assertion, pro
cation of something that is true. I think of pra
ment about behavior and affirmation as mor
validation of one's being.

In parenting, there is a distinction betwe
do and affirming who they are. Perfectio

ral gifts and pointing them out, taking an interest in things they love, getting to know them by being with them, and listening.

The combination of praise and affirmation helps children to develop self-worth. Praise alone deprives us of good feelings about ourselves. Working only for praise is akin to chasing a carrot that you never get to eat. It is painful to be loved only when you are meeting the needs of a parent.

Violation of Boundaries

Healthy boundaries help us to feel safe. They make it possible for us to be intimate without losing ourselves in the process. When we are raised by parents who do not know how to set boundaries, abuse and victimization may be the result. Examples of subtle violations of boundaries by parents are as follows:

- Role reversals. Janet's mother said with pride, "Janet and I are very close. I can tell her anything. We are like sisters." Children need parents to be parents. Many parents tell their children about their adult problems or allow them to overhear their worries. Some may even seek support from the child.
- Smothering, kissing, hugging, or other physical contact without the child's approval.
- Hovering and inserting themselves into their children's lives beyond what is comfortable for the children.
- Telling children what they like, how they feel, when they are hungry, and what their needs are without input from the child.
- Lack of privacy or personal space.
- Enmeshment or forced togetherness with family members.
- Adult-centered families, in which the parents' needs and preferences are the only ones considered. Children are ignored or seen as little adults.

Repression of Feelings

In families with the potential for severe abuse, it is a wise choice to keep feelings hidden. In mildly dysfunctional families, there is no need to repress feelings or to be afraid of violence; however, in such families the rules of several generations of painful families may continue to apply.

When an appropriate expression of feelings is not modeled or permitted, children are left with handicaps in many areas of their lives. The members of a looking-good family appear to be in control and may even look happy. Every human being has both positive and negative emotions. If anger, fear, or sadness are never acknowledged, we can only assume that painful feelings are hidden just beneath the glossy surface.

Being unable to identify or express feelings prevents us from connecting in an intimate way with other human beings. Feelings are our compass: our anger guides us to action, if we listen to it; grief, if honored, helps us to recover and learn from our losses; fear both protects us and dares us to face it and move through; shame tries to protect us, but we need to face it and come out of the darkness to overcome its negative influence on our lives.

Compulsive behavior and stress-related illness are also worsened, if not directly caused, by the repression of feelings. Stomach problems, headaches, or sleep disturbance can become a problem for life.

I like to look at the way we learn to manage emotions from the perspective of "pre-Oprah" parenting and "post-Oprah" parenting. Before parents had the kind of experts who appeared on *The Oprah Winfrey Show*, self-help books, educational television programs, access to quality counseling, or even the cultural permission to seek help, they did the best they could with what they had. Well-intentioned parents may have had access to the writings of Dr. Spock but certainly not as widely as we have today with television programs and Internet access. Unfortunately, they often lacked the skills and tools to show their children how to address feelings. I think we are all doing a better job today, but there is a long way to go. There is help for those who seek it.

The Process of Stage 1

The identification stage tends to begin on a high note, generating some relief from shame, the knowledge that we are not alone, and a sense of hope—knowing that there is a path to follow. A shift occurs midway in stage 1 when we gain an understanding about our past and how much there is to learn. "Stepping down off the pedestal" is a sobering experience, and a new stage of integrating and practicing what we have learned begins.

Although we can see more clearly what is wrong and we have some sense of what needs to change, we are still not seeing the changes. The next step will take a great leap of faith in order to move from an intellectual awareness of your problems to truly changing and healing; it will mean going through it.

STAGE 2: BECOMING ME

You are great at your core. Your essence was and is exactly who you are meant to be. It's just a matter of remembering it and bringing it forward. You might also have to locate a few parts of your essence that you may have left behind. Once you gather them up, you will need to love your essence and bring it into a permanent place in your life.

Next you will need to introduce all of your loved ones to your essence, giving them time to get used to the idea. You may also have to take it to work and see if it matches what you are doing. If not, you may need to rethink your career plans. After all that work, you can relax a little and enjoy being you and growing for the rest of your life.

The second stage in the process is that of developing authenticity and vulnerability. Perfectionists spend a lifetime trying to avoid being exposed, letting their feelings show, making mistakes, or being found out. Believe it or not, these things will be good for you. This stage cannot be bypassed.

Essence is always a good thing. It is a person's spirit, temperament, personality, gifts, and interests blended together. It makes us who we are. We are unique but not separate from others. I see essence as the perfect design for an individual's life purpose. We can go in any number of directions using our essence, but we will find peace only if we are authentic.

Chapter 2 explained the process of adapting to the experience of early childhood when attachment is interrupted or inconsistent. In order to stay connected for our own survival, we needed to exaggerate some of our strongest traits and minimize or hide others. We created a pseudo-self in the context of our families, influenced by events that affected our parents even before we were born. We are designed to be able to adjust in order to survive physically and emotionally. Unfortunately, the resulting pattern is now the problem to be faced.

There are things you know about yourself that you are certain are true that may actually be adaptations you made in childhood. When I ask clients in a group how they would describe themselves as children, they almost always answer with traits they exhibited as teenagers. Those years are easier to recall and usually have some turmoil that might have left scars. Yet essence is not found by reflecting on your adolescence. That is a time of trial and error, peer influences, and a break from norms.

To find your essence, you have to look at your younger years, before age ten. It is important to look at yourself from a neutral perspective. For example, some might say that a child is too sensitive. Sensitivity is a trait that is full of positive potential at birth. No one is born too sensitive. Nor is a child born controlling. He or she may be a leader, kind, or cautious, but not controlling.

It isn't necessary to have memories to find your essence, because your body and your spirit remember who you are. To answer "Who are you?" you must feel your way through the question, sensing more than thinking.

Try to answer the following questions about yourself under the age of ten. Don't think too much, just write. (I have put my own answers in parentheses as examples.)

- When I was little, I loved ______________________________
  (to swing by myself and sing)
- I always wished that I could ____________________________
  (fly)
- I dreamed of being ___________________________________
  (a writer, a dancer)
- My raw talents are ____________________________________
  (twirling baton, talking)
- In a group, at school, or with friends I was ________________
  (a leader, talker, active)
- My family would say that I was __________________________
  (sensitive, attention seeking, awkward)

- Physically I was ______________________________
  (tall, skinny)
- I sometimes struggled with ______________________
  (saying the wrong thing or talking too much at school)
- With my siblings I ___________________________
  (felt stuck in the middle, less than)
- I was afraid of _____________________________
  (heights, anger, new things like swimming, the dentist)
- I often felt ________________________________
  (that I didn't fit in well, scared)

Common Childhood Traits

Circle the traits that you think applied to you as a child:

Serious	A risk taker	An intravert
Sweet	Busy	A little adult
Kind	Athletic	Pretty
Funny	Shy	Handsome
Active	Sociable	A singer
Cautious	A leader	A dancer
Impulsive	Helpful	Cute
Outgoing	Smiley	Compassionate
Talkative	Loving	Quiet
Bright	A dreamer	Smart
Curious	Fearless	Enthusiastic
Affectionate	An extrovert	Passionate

Review the items you circled and notice the traits you had when you were young that you (1) used as a way of coping, or (2) gave up or hid away because they were not working in your family.

Your Emotions as a Child

After each statement, circle any responses that you think fit best for you or add your own response, if you need to.

- WHEN SOMEONE HURT MY FEELINGS, I WOULD:

Cry
Hide
Get angry
Lash out
Feel ashamed
Go to my mother or my father
Tell someone

- IF I HURT SOMEONE'S FEELINGS, I WOULD:

Cry
Deny it
Try not to care about it
Hurt myself
Feel ashamed
Turn to someone for help
Apologize
Get angry

- WHEN I WAS SCARED, I WOULD:

Pretend I wasn't
Cry
Run away
Help someone else
Tell my mother or my father
Hold it inside
Feel sick

Get angry

Tell someone else

Get quiet

- I WAS HAPPY WHEN I WAS:

With friends

Alone

With my parent(s)

With my sibling(s)

Playing outside

In my room

Away from home

At home

- WHEN I WAS HAPPY, I:

Talked more

Was full of energy

Kept it to myself

Smiled

Laughed

Shared it with others

- WHEN I FELT SAD, I WOULD:

Cry

Want to be alone

Go to my mother or my father

Tell a friend

Write

Try to distract myself

Get busy playing

Help someone

- WHEN I WAS ANGRY, I WOULD:
  Cry
  Hurt someone or something
  Hurt myself
  Run away
  Feel ashamed
  Hide
  Deny it
  Find a distraction
  Talk about it
  Say nothing
- IF MY PARENT WAS UPSET WITH ME, I WOULD:
  Cry
  Say I was sorry
  Run away
  Feel ashamed
  Feel alone and sad
  Promise to be better
  Get angry
  Blame someone else
  Try not to care
  Hate myself

Look back over this list and ask yourself how you may be the same or different today, in an adult context.

Your Gifts and Strengths

It is important to notice that the same traits that caused you to struggle are often the greatest assets you have. The traits below have been reported by others as their gifts and strengths. Circle those that apply, even in part, to you as a child.

Talkative	Coordinated
A singer	A pleasing personality
A dreamer	Good-looking
Artistic	Energetic
Creative	Outspoken
Courageous	Forthright
Intelligent	Athletic
Beautiful	Persistent
A dancer	Sensitive
Physically strong	Generous
Emotionally strong	Empathetic
Resilient	Intuitive
Optimistic	Loyal
Has faith	Loves animals
Compassionate	Enthusiastic

Look at your choices and notice the traits that are part of your life now and also those that may have slipped into the background. Add your own if they are not on the list. Are there any gifts that you want to bring back? Are there some you would want to give up or modify in some way?

Your Challenges and Weaknesses

I have always had to curb my enthusiasm and watch out for my impulsiveness. Those two traits combined got me into some trouble in the past and could still surface today. I have always been a talker, and if I don't think before I talk, I can make a mess of things. Challenges like this are not character defects. When things go badly, it is usually the result of a combination of things, such as how much we used our gift, the timing, and the mood we were in at the time. How troublesome a trait becomes may also depend on whether your parents were able to help you to learn how to manage it. In adulthood, counseling can be a great help with that.

Sensitivity is a great example of a gift that can cause problems if we don't have the guidance to manage it. The reason many parents see it as a flaw is that they become very anxious when their child is upset, and they fear that their child will have a terrible life with all those feelings. It is possible to develop a set of tools that can be used when emotions become intense. That would include a support system, books and articles that you can read, faith, prayer, meditation, self-love, physical exercise, and talking about it with someone. I do most of those things myself, and I find that authors Wayne Dyer and Marianne Williamson, among others, often turn my mind to a positive direction.

Everyone has traits that are great and not so great in his or her essence. Judging your essence as bad can paralyze you with shame. Accepting that you do not need to change your essence will take the sting out of making mistakes.

Coming Out: Taking the Show on the Road

Once you have taken a good unbiased look at your essence, you have to take another leap of faith and take the show on the road. Remember that the only goal is to improve your quality of life. This includes having peace of mind, being able to form lasting relationships, using your gifts and talents for the betterment of your life and of others, being a loving and effective parent (if you have children), and being able to have satisfying and successful intimate relationships throughout your life. Shame and fear will try to prevent you from doing this, but there are ways to work around that.

You may have heard the expression "Feel the fear and do it anyway." I would say, "Feel the fear, guilt, and shame and do it anyway." I include guilt for those who have trouble distinguishing it from shame. All three of these feelings drive us into a defensive posture, away from the things we love, and toward compulsive behaviors. When you decide to take the step of coming out, you must be prepared for all three.

As a perfectionist "steps down off the chair," he or she is flooded with painful thoughts and self-doubt. Shame tells us, "What must people think of me?" "I'm a mess and now they know." "How can I face my boss after I challenged him at a staff meeting?" Fear says, "No one is going to want to be around me, knowing I'm weak and depressed." "What will happen if I tell my sister I don't want to hear her complain anymore? My whole family will be mad at me." Guilt says, "I can't abandon my friends who depend on me. I feel selfish and mean."

Under all that is a bigger question: "Who am I if I give all of this up?" With the extra time and energy you have when you are not managing and controlling everything, you may be able to find the answer. The shocking reality is that if people love you and really care, they will be happy to see you "off the chair." They want to know who you are.

It is awkward at first when you begin to let them know that you have needs and feelings as well as a bad day or a problem you need help with. Some of those people have been feeling distant from you for a long time and want to be equals with you. The problems of others (not your own) have most likely been the focal point in these relationships. Your job was to supply the answers.

Shame is sometimes an invisible saboteur in our lives. It is important to know what your shame feels like and how to identify it quickly. Once you identify shame as the source of your discomfort, you can do something to intervene and manage it more effectively than you have in the past. The only alternative to facing it is to relapse into your unwanted patterns to cover it up.

Most perfectionists are not even aware of what I call a "shame attack" and do not have the language to describe it. People use words like *sick*, *devastated*, *bad*, *crushed*, or *worthless* to describe the feeling. They are depressed, withdrawn, and silent in response to some thought or incident, not knowing why and not able to identify how it happened or how to get out of it.

The feeling of shame makes us want to hide, to go inside ourselves and retreat from the world. It is a sense of extreme vulnerability coupled with an inability to cope with further wounding. We feel exposed, caught with our flaws showing, and we think that the world (or maybe just one person) now knows how truly "bad" we are. Another version is feeling misunderstood and deeply upset about what someone thinks of us, even if it is not true. Our own imagination can create a shame attack by thinking of something painful from the past.

Shame attacks can occur even when we did not actually do anything wrong. We are in pain because of the disapproval of someone who matters. Withdrawing from the world actually makes the shame increase. Like a mold, shame grows faster without sunlight. The antidote for shame is coming out of the dark: describing your shame to someone who is safe and working it through. The longer we are silent, the more the shame is internalized, and we eventually forget the source entirely but keep the pain. Therapists can be safe supports and guides, but since you have to pay them, the unconditional support of friends and loved ones is meaningful on a deeper level.

Antidotes for a Shame Attack

- **Externalize.** Shame acts like a virus that comes from nowhere and attacks. It can be fought. Say to yourself, *I am not my shame. It is a feeling that will pass.*
- **Identify the shame attack quickly and name it.** The longer it has a chance to take hold, the harder it is to fight back. As soon as you know it is shame, say so!
- **Come out.** Don't hide from safe people. Tell someone who cares about you how you feel. Talk about the feeling more than the cause. Knowing why may not help you feel better.
- **Read helpful writings or listen to helpful speakers.** Wayne Dyer's and Marianne Williamson's books have helped me. Keep handy anything that has helped you before and read or listen over and over, if necessary, instead of obsessing or analyzing what you did wrong or what you are upset about.
- **Temporarily stay away from "trigger" people or situations until your pain has passed.** Any risky person is going to increase the pain. Don't confront anyone, and save the serious discussions for later.
- **While you're in the midst of a shame attack, don't trust your own thoughts.** They are probably all negative and distorted by the pain. Try not to take yourself too seriously until the pain goes away. It is the shame talking, and it will pass.
- **Postpone major decisions or responsibilities until you are in better shape.** Usually this will be just a day or two. Don't act on the pain, no matter how strongly you want to lash out or take action. Healthy people don't retaliate in their relationships. If you act out, you may create another problem that you will have to undo later.

- **Visualize yourself giving back any of the shame that does not belong to you.** For example, imagine returning negative messages to those who gave them to you (e.g., parents, partners, bosses). Ask yourself honestly, *Which part of the criticism do I need to own?* Shrink it into a manageable size and give the rest back (in your mind). Even the worst criticism is usually partly true.
- **Put energy into self-caring until you feel less vulnerable.** Go outdoors, put your bare feet in the grass, take walks, pray, breathe, exercise, buy yourself flowers, or get a massage.
- **Once the shame has lifted, notice your patterns and your progress.** Ask yourself, *How did I get into this? What was helpful or not? Who or what made it worse? Did I get over it faster than the last time? Is there anything I need to change in my life or relationships?*

The Goal

If you consistently practice for several years, the episodes will be less and less frequent, and you will be able to stop them within hours or even minutes. The stages of identification and coming out are never fully complete. Perfectionists don't like that. Remember the goal: quality of life, not winning.

STAGE 3: LETTING GO AND FORGIVING

The stage of letting go and forgiving may be simultaneous with stages 1 and 2. During the third stage, you will spend more time working on changing your thoughts and behaviors. If you don't know much about your essence, this will be difficult to do.

Although it is definitely hard work to make permanent changes in the way we live, this stage is much less painful than the previous two. Long-term change is a matter of learning, practicing, and integrating new ways of living. This is a time of becoming congruent—of thoughts, feelings, and actions working together. For everything we let go of, there is something new and better to replace it. There are losses and new beginnings. This stage is more about living than about surviving and healing. Using a support system helps to prevent backsliding and reminds us who we once were and who we would like to become.

Once you have experienced and taken responsibility for your own pain, you will reach a point where you are at peace within yourself about how you arrived here. There is no need to blame or focus on your family or past relationships as the source of your problems.

In this stage, you might feel a new connection to your history and feel humbled and blessed to have had the rare opportunity of deep personal change. With it comes an increasing sense of awe in this process and gratitude for what has been learned and gained from the pain of the past. There is a strong belief that you can change anything you desire to change about who you are today. There is no need to focus on the past unless it has lessons to teach you.

Letting Go

Letting go encompasses the following:

- We no longer try to change others, or if we do, we quickly realize the futility of it.
- We let go of blame and anger that are part of a victim role we no longer need to play.
- We gradually begin to enjoy being "out of control"

while we learn to use our personal and spiritual power.

- We place others, including our children, in the hands of a higher power while we strive to be as healthy in our relationships as we can be at this point in our lives.
- We let go of the future, striving to live in the moment and looking ahead only to plan our actions, not the outcomes or our feelings.
- We slowly let go of fantasies about how things should have been and begin to live and accept the way things are.

Forgiveness of Self and Others

Amends are made as we undo old hurts by being the best selves we can be today. It is a necessary step, since we are all human and even perfectionists make regrettable mistakes. Sometimes saying "I'm sorry" will make a difference. But more often, we must prove over time that we can be trusted and that we really have changed. The best thing we can do for others is to be the healthiest we know how to be, treating others as we would like to be treated, no matter what their reactions.

RITA'S STORY

Rita's story is one to which many can relate. At forty-four, she had two sons—Josh, sixteen, and Mark, fourteen—and a daughter Lily, age ten. She had just remarried after divorcing the children's father two years before I met her. Her history, like many others, was that of a difficult childhood, but as a bright, motivated middle child, Rita got through it by doing her best to stay under the radar, away from conflict, and planning her escape after high school.

During the divorce, Rita sought counseling for a few months for herself and her children and began to build a new life as a single mother. She focused on her family and wanted to do the right things to help her children adjust. There was no time to examine her marriage or herself.

Despite her best efforts, her children did not seem to be doing well. They had always been obedient and well-mannered children. Their home was neat and orderly, homework and chores were done, and they all got along.

Josh had taken it hard when his father moved out, however, and resented having to go back and forth for visitation. At sixteen, he also resented his mother's control: dictating his bedtime, hovering over him doing his homework, and forcing him into activities he didn't choose, like cross-country running. Mark was a loner, overweight, and glued to his computer, which she monitored closely. Mark's father had given him the computer and a few video games that she did not approve of. Lily was an anxious child who worried about her mother and father and wanted them to be together.

The children did not bond with her new husband, Carl. He didn't talk to them the way their father had, and he tried to discipline them, which they resented.

Rita's fears about her family falling apart with the new arrangement only increased over the early months of their marriage. She and Carl were arguing: he complained about the children, and she withdrew. She was in pain. She believed that she had failed in her first marriage, derailed her children's lives, and now had made a huge mistake in remarrying.

Her biggest challenge was within herself, and not the practical problems she was facing. Many people get through similar situations and eventually adjust with a little help. Rita could not forgive herself for making "selfish" choices that hurt her children. She was ashamed that she was divorced and feared that this relationship was failing, too. Before she divorced, she looked perfect; now she couldn't face her friends or family without feeling like a disgrace.

In our sessions, we worked on the first two stages, including her childhood and her essence. She learned that she had been a perfectionist in her first marriage, which she thought may have contributed to her husband having an affair. She was critical and didn't allow him to fully participate in raising the children. Now she was expecting her children to make her proud and be perfect, too. They were resisting her control, and so was her new husband.

The changes she needed to make would be subtle and were all about letting go. She accomplished a great deal by doing less and allowing everyone else to find his or her own way. With the help of couples counseling, Rita could see that the more she stayed out of the middle, the better her husband got along with her children. What an awakening it was for Rita to discover that by doing less she was accomplishing more!

The hardest part of her process was forgiving herself for the mistakes she had made. Rita initially felt defensive. She minimized her perfectionism and justified it by saying that her ex-husband wouldn't help, so she had to do everything alone. Eventually she saw the benefits for everyone when she shared responsibility and accepted her current husband as he was. She regretted—and apologized to her children for—being so critical of their father, and she was starting to let go of her resentment toward him.

She was happy that Lily would have a few more years with the experience of a loving family. There was a chance that her children would struggle with ongoing issues because of their experience, but Rita knew that her controlling and worrying wouldn't prevent that, either. She needed to trust that she would know what to do if that time came.

Summary

In this chapter, we took a closer look at what is good about perfectionism and weighed that against the downside. That should have helped to strengthen your commitment to change. The first step in the process of making that change is identifying the problem. This stage begins with awareness and takes a closer look at the past and the experiences that may have led you to this point. It is uncomfortable but worth the effort.

In the second stage, becoming yourself, you took a look at your essence and set the course for coming out as an authentic, vulnerable human being. The third step, letting go and forgiving, is a stage of deeper change and honesty with yourself and others about what you regret and who you want to be. These stages overlap, and the process can continue as you grow throughout life.

Chapter 7

Making Your Life Easier with Acceptance and Humor

Picture your life with one major change: you are able to love and accept people as they are, starting with yourself. Imagine waking up tomorrow morning with no critical thoughts or judgments of those around you. Perfectionists would be baffled by that idea, but ironically, they would also say that they wish that others would accept *them* as they are. We all want that very much. So how would that day be different? We would be forced to look at what *is* and decide to embrace it.

My husband and I are very different people. I jokingly say that he is a manatee and I am a dolphin. We are both lovable and beautiful people, but I move fast and rarely stop, whereas he hangs around and makes our world a better place with his easy personality and his love for our children. While I am hurrying to get to the next thing, he takes time to be friendly and has long, deep conversations with those he cares about and some whom he barely knows. If I focused on our differences as a negative, I would probably complain about how much I do around the house and that it isn't equal or fair. Eventually I would resent him and magnify his flaws, which would most likely cause him to do the same to me, and we would have a very strained relationship.

I have dealt with our differences both ways: sometimes urging him to be more like me and at other times loving him for who he is and keeping my eye off the differences. Guess which works better? I learned long ago that where I focus is really a choice. If I stare at what is wrong or upsetting in the world or in my house, I feel agitated, irritable, and justified. It gets bigger and bigger until I find myself feeling alone and bitter. The other choice is the sort of day I mentioned above, when I decide to accept people the way they are. I feel lighter and happier, and I laugh more. I am more loving, and I get more love. I am calm in traffic and enjoy the people I work with even when I'm not fond of my duties that day.

Do we really want people to be just like us? Imagine that for a moment. I don't think that would work very well. I certainly wouldn't want my husband to have my temperament. Sometimes I can't deal with it in myself! Perfectionists who are driven by their own anxiety, fear, and shame become obsessed with right and wrong and with tasks and activities rather than with the people they care about. Instead of letting go, they push harder to do more. They worry about the future or their own failures and are not *here* now.

THE PARADOX OF ACCEPTANCE

Why don't we accept people, especially those we love, all the time? Fear is the biggest reason. Once again, imagine that day of pure acceptance. If we accept others, doesn't that mean that they are getting away with being imperfect? If we didn't complain, there would be no negative consequences and they would continue their methods undeterred. It's not fair! When we are consistently irritated by the lack of perfection in someone else, it is often because we are jealous and perturbed that they can relax and take care of themselves or that they don't worry about being perfect and getting everything done.

A good way to test this theory when you are irritated is to ask yourself, *What is it that I don't have that I really need in this situation?* (Think hard and go deep.) The answer may be as simple as *I want to relax* or *I want to play*. If so, try doing it. You are responsible for your own use of energy, and if you need rest, get it, regardless of what someone else is doing. On the other hand, if it is a situation that you can make better by taking action, or communicating, do that. If it is about a personal need that you can address by taking care of yourself, do that. In most cases, our loved ones do not have to change for us to be okay.

Perfectionists, if they are honest, have to admit that using disapproval and criticism to punish those who are not as "good" as those of us who are almost perfect just doesn't work. Acceptance is much more likely to inspire someone to want to please us, but it won't work if it is disguised as putting up with, being resigned to, or ignoring the person. In order for acceptance to be believed, it has to be authentic and based on love, without a need for approval.

The paradox is that the best way to ensure that you will be accepted as you are is to accept the ones you love the way *they* are. It sounds easy, but it isn't, really. There are some complaints or requests for change that are legitimate. This is where we have to look at the temperament and traits of the person with whom we have a conflict. An individual cannot change his or her essence. People can moderate and try harder to shift their behavior in the direction of your needs, but they may fail or be inconsistent.

One of the silliest things that partners say to each other when they are frustrated is "If you loved me, you would change." The fact that someone is unable to change for us has nothing to do with love. One frequent example is the issue of lateness. There are some people who have been late since they were born. People who are late are generally late. That is one of the traits that is usually a lifetime challenge and not an attempt to control other people. Many who are among the late are loving, considerate partners who would change if they could. I can hear the perfectionists groaning as I write this.

Let's turn it around, then. If you were born with a tendency toward organization and a preference for order, it is probably still with you. I have trouble walking out of any room without picking up clutter, cups, papers, mail, and so on. This annoys members of my family, who would like me to leave things alone, and they often blame my "cleaning frenzies" for their lost items. This trait of mine isn't going to change, however—not because I think I'm right but because I really can't change it. It is part of who I am. It helps if we remember that there are many things in each of us that bother other people, yet we are not able to change. Behaviors may change, but inborn traits don't.

This presents another paradox. You must accept yourself as you are in order to change. If you cannot change your essence (e.g., I will always have a tendency to be overly busy, independent, and an optimist), what can you change to better yourself? The challenge is to become very self-aware while focusing on maximizing your strengths and moderating your troublesome traits to the best of your ability. The greatest change occurs when you become conscious of your emotions and begin to choose how you react to the people and situations in your life. Eventually, these changes—in perspective (e.g., increased acceptance of yourself and others)—bring about a healthier response to problems or conflicts and will make a huge difference in your quality of life and relationships.

If you are in a relationship with someone who you fear will use this approach as an excuse not to change something that is very important to you, don't despair. You have to start by choosing well and making sure you have a partner who wants what is best for both of you. The bottom line is that behaviors like respect, kindness, generosity, honesty, loyalty, and fidelity are good things to expect and cannot be negotiated. These essentials may even require improvement at times, but they must be there in the first place. These things are related to love and the character of the person involved. I could not accept my husband as he is if we did not share these values in our relationship.

What about legitimate concerns that are bothering you? Even if you work diligently to be accepting, there will be issues that come up in any relationship in which needs conflict. Acceptance does not mean that you won't ever be upset or complain, it just means that you won't dwell on it daily and criticize regularly. It is wise to have a talk about the hot topic—for example, the mess that has been in the corner for three months or your request that your sister call you once in a while.

Your loved one needs to know how you feel about the issue, and you can hope that this time something might change, but also try not to get obsessed or hung up on it. If you can let it go, that's great; if you can't, and it is making you resentful, take action yourself out of love, not as a way to demonstrate your superiority. Clean up the corner or call your sister!

Another paradox of acceptance is that when there is a frequent, plentiful exchange of love, gratitude, compliments, and attachment behaviors in general, we aren't bothered by the trivia. Even if nothing changes except that there is more love, we can be happy and laugh about what we don't like. We can actually be happy whenever we think loving thoughts about the people in our lives.

Just like every other emotion, happiness comes and goes; it is not a permanent state to strive for. Even the feeling of love comes and goes. We can love someone and not like him or her much today or maybe lose sexual interest temporarily. Love can return if we are able to catch the critical voice and turn it around.

LOVING A PERFECTIONIST

Some readers have chosen to read this book because they are in a close relationship with a perfectionist who is reluctant to change. The list below will be important for you. But before you get to that, I'd like to provide some guidance and suggestions specifically for your situation. By now, you understand that perfectionism is a pattern based in part on temperament. That part is permanent, so your first task is to begin to practice acceptance of your loved one as he or she is.

Your second task is to examine the ways that you have been accommodating the perfectionist in your life. This is a good example of how it sometimes becomes a problem for the nonperfectionist.

Helen, age thirty-eight, was a client I saw a few years ago who was married to a perfectionist named Jack, age forty-three. Helen had started out in her marriage as a relaxed and slightly disorganized person who actually saw her husband's need for order as an asset. She was a bit sloppy and not great with money. Jack was very disciplined himself, and she thought that this would make her a better person. He was glad that she wanted to change. They decided not to have a child, which was a choice Helen had pretty much made for herself before she met Jack. They put their resources and energy into buying and decorating the "perfect" home for just the two of them.

Helen had always planned to get a golden retriever—it had been a dream of hers since childhood—but Jack kept putting it off. She also liked to entertain and wanted to have regular book club meetings at their home, but Jack didn't like the mess that made or the inconvenience to him of having to get out of the house when her friends were there. So Helen didn't have a dog and didn't hold book club meetings in her "perfect" house. These were just a few of the examples Helen described at our first meeting.

After a few years, she noticed that she was staying late at work and was reluctant to come home. She went to the movies alone and spent every Saturday with her family because Jack didn't want to join her. She started to think that she was no longer herself and had given in more than was good for her. She was giving in out of fear of Jack's disapproval and moodiness, and her resentment was building. She asked Jack to join her for couples counseling, but he was not willing to do that—at least, not at first.

Helen wanted the marriage to work, but she was headed in the wrong direction by staying away and avoiding conflict. That approach would definitely end the relationship. She had also been assuming that Jack was incapable of change and unwilling to try.

I worked with Helen on identifying what her values and desires had been before she met Jack compared to what they were now. She could do that, but she was afraid to speak up and face his moods. She needed help and some support from friends to take the necessary steps to tell Jack who she was and what she wanted. Jack did not have to change for Helen to feel better. She could take steps to simply find her place in their home and their marriage. Helen's biggest goal was to get a dog.

After a few months, Helen asked Jack to go to couples counseling, and he agreed to see a therapist I recommended. I continued to see Helen periodically to help her with being assertive and identifying her needs. Jack remained a committed perfectionist, as far as I know, but Helen has a dog.

The point is to be yourself and own your space in the relationship. If you need help to identify your needs and assert yourself, *get help*. It is okay to be disorganized and sloppy at times, even when there is a perfectionist in the house. You may need to intercede for your children if they are being bullied into compliance with the perfectionist's need for order.

The tips below apply to any situation in which you feel the need to change someone else, but the loved one is not ready for change:

1. **Stop giving advice.** Sometimes you think you are just helping, but advice can be demeaning and habit-forming, and it doesn't foster closeness, only dependency. Even when you are asked for advice, think twice. Try just saying, "Gosh, that's a tough problem," "I really don't know what I would do," "I think you will find an answer eventually," or "I believe in you"—or say nothing.
2. **Be honest and share feelings.** This requires self-awareness and timing. Confrontations don't work. Ask yourself why you want or need the person to join you or approach life the same way you do. What is the unmet need underneath it all? It could be that you want to be one-up in the relationship for a change or that you need to be closer to your friend or loved

one. If that is the case, just say you want to be closer. Don't try to convince the other person to be like you.

3. **Let moments of connection come to you.** Remember the paradox that less is more. If you relax and accept those you love, they are more likely to open up to you. When you force a conversation, they will probably shut down and distance themselves from you.
4. **Work on authenticity.** Be you, be real. Perfectionism and looking good get in the way of intimacy.
5. **Avoid jargon, slogans, and preaching.** This includes handing out self-help books. If you integrate what *you* learn from books (be the book!), you may be surprised when someone asks you where you learned that. *Then* you can give him or her the book. Attraction is better than aggressive promotion.
6. **Build trust by listening, loving, and accepting others as they are.** This is the best way to show people that you are a safe and loving person. If they ever decide that they want to change, they will surely let you know.
7. **Set gentle limits when necessary.** Acceptance doesn't mean tolerating unacceptable behavior in your relationships. If you need something, speak up. Here is an example: "When you complain about your husband to me, I don't enjoy our time together. Let's talk about something else." It may be hard for people to change, so you might have to remind them once in a while or step back from the relationship if it continues.
8. **Have faith in love.** Don't underestimate your loved ones' abilities to gradually accept your growth and choices.

It takes time to refurbish the way you conduct yourself

in a relationship, but over the years you may find that even though your loved ones have not changed in other relationships, they are healthier with you. Enjoy that.

BRINGING HUMOR INTO LIFE

Humor has many known benefits for short- and long-term health, happiness, satisfaction with life, work, parenting, and intimate relationships. An active sense of humor is a sign that we are letting go of control, balancing the scales of stress, and feeling more content with life as it is. As we move away from pain and anxiety, we need to learn to laugh more and find humor anywhere we can. Laughter is a genuine expression of the joy we feel internally in the moment. A stressful situation or a serious problem may even have a funny side to it.

We can benefit from association with those who help us to see the humor in life. I am blessed to have a very funny family of Irish descent who love to tell stories, often at their own expense. Those are the best. Whenever a trying situation arises, someone will often say, "This will make a good story someday!"—and it does. Perfectionists have trouble laughing at themselves, and it is a true sign of growth when they can.

Beware of humor that is really anger in disguise. Sarcasm, cynicism, and teasing are hurtful ways of one-upping others. Work on finding the humor that is pure joy and does not have a negative undertone.

Your essence also dictates the type of humor you will enjoy. The TV show *America's Funniest Home Videos* provides videos that are not only funny but, for some, therapeutic. *The Office* is hilarious to my adult children, but I don't always get it. The sitcom *Modern Fam-*

ily is my current favorite and makes me laugh every time I see it. It is even funny to talk about it with others who enjoy it. The laughs last longer that way.

In the "work now, play later" world of perfectionism, you might not laugh very often, but today it is fairly easy to find humor in your e-mail inbox, on YouTube (I like babies and puppies), on TV sitcoms, in old favorite movies (e.g., *Airplane*), or on Comedy Central. Start making a list of things that you know will make you laugh, and use them deliberately as an antidepressant or a stress buster, rather than waiting for humor to come to you. If you are lucky enough to have children or grandchildren, they can be a great resource. Ask for face time or get videos you can play when the mood strikes.

FINDING ROLE MODELS OF COURAGE

The most courageous thing a perfectionist can do is to reveal who he or she is spontaneously. Some covert perfectionists may appear to be doing that, but it is sometimes just an effort to hide their vulnerability by putting themselves down with humor. Occasionally, I see men or women who are obviously comfortable with themselves and who take risks without thinking. My aunt Ann is one of those people. Now in her eighties, she has a bright personality, with red hair to match. Every time I have seen her throughout my life, she has run up to me and said loudly, "*Annie!*" She laughs louder than anyone else and tells stories about my father as a child that I thoroughly enjoy. She has had serious problems in her life that could inhibit her, but she doesn't let that happen. I smile every time I think of her.

I had an aunt on my mother's side who was also a great role model, especially for humor. Years ago, when my aunt Shirley was dying from ovarian cancer, she wrote a letter about how she was getting along. In it she said, "I was out riding through the woods on my golf cart the other day, and I lost my wig. I didn't even know it until I went to check it to see if it was straight. I found it hanging on a branch of a tree! Now I use double-stick rug tape. If it sticks to my head before I get it straight, I end up wearing the ear flap on my forehead all day!" She died a few months later, but before she passed away, she picked out a wife for her husband, knowing he would need one.

My mother, now eighty-six (she will be upset that I'm telling you that), has had a hard life, especially as a child. She is smart, funny, and clever. When I asked my father last year what I should get her for Christmas, he said, "Oh, just get her anything with a plug, and she'll play with it for hours." She loves to tinker and can face a computer head-on, fearlessly talking to techies on the phone in the middle of the night, if she has to. She is in my corner always. She makes me feel better than I am. I am so proud to be her daughter. She wants me to write another book about my crazy life. I might just do that.

My closest friend, Marilyn, at seventy-nine, is a fabulous role model for hundreds of women and has been with me in my work and my personal life for more than twenty-five years. She is my cheerleader, confidante, mentor, and consultant, and I would not be me without her. After having nine children, Marilyn decided, at age fifty, to start a career as a therapist. She worked hard at it, and her natural abilities were remarkable, so in no time she had built up a clientele. Thousands of people have changed their lives because of her. Her example of how to balance work and fun gives me a road map for who I want to be.

I also have three wonderful, lively, loving, and loyal sisters. I know what a blessing that is. We are very different, and because of that, we balance one another well. They always make me laugh and are perfectly willing to cry with me. It wasn't always that way, mostly because I wouldn't let them. We all have worked on our issues, and we have become more attached throughout the years. I'm never really alone, with them in my corner. My father made sure we all had good educations and used our abilities, and we have

The women above are the women I want to be when I grow up.

If you want to loosen up, become more spontaneous, and laugh more, you will need to find people who can demonstrate how it is done, and then let them. Whom do you admire and desire to emulate? Whom do you lean on when you are shaky? Dare to get close enough to others and allow them to influence you. Listen to their stories. Watch what they do when a storm hits. Ask for their help. Use their gifts along with your own.

BUILDING A STRONG SUPPORT SYSTEM

I certainly hope that by now we are past the old message that being in therapy is a sign of weakness. Getting help and needing support are now "cool," and going to counseling doesn't mean you are damaged or defective. I'm in favor of doing whatever it takes to get you in a healthier state faster. Perfectionists may still say, "What can they tell me that I don't already know?" The answer is that trained clinical professionals can hold up a mirror for you to see what you cannot see for yourself.

The formula that I believe works best is a combination of self-help books, counseling or therapy, and a strong and ongoing support system. Today it is possible to find twelve-step groups that meet almost any need you have, any day of the week, and at no cost. There are always new online support groups for women, for men, or for both that target specific issues. Some are even set up in a format that encourages the creating of local support groups. Churches and other houses of worship often provide topical support groups as well.

If you already have some strong friendships or sibling relationships, it is probably time to start using them. Perfectionists often stay in the strong role with those around them. You may have friends and family members who have been waiting for you to open up and relax a little. Turn to them for support and ask for help when you need it.

FINDING THE RIGHT GUIDES FOR YOUR JOURNEY

There are many ways to recover and many people and programs to help you along the way. Rule number one is to go where you feel safe and connected. There is no right way, despite what some professionals believe. It doesn't matter where you begin. In fact, many individuals have actually begun recovery long before they are consciously aware of it. Reading and seeking new ideas and information is one way to remain noncommittal while testing the waters. Perfectionists may tend to stay there a bit too long, however, wanting to make sure they know everything before they take any chances.

Counseling or Therapy

The terms *counseling* and *therapy* are generally used interchangeably. Following is a list of things to look for when you seek professional help, based on my own professional experience and the voices of others who have been successful:

1. A good reputation based on long-term experience is the best reference a therapist or a program can offer. *New* doesn't mean *bad*, but it may be best to listen to friends who are

familiar with the quality of the service.

2. Many people think that certain credentials are better than others. If there are mental health issues involved that require diagnosis and possibly medication, a psychiatrist *and* a psychotherapist would be advisable. Most psychiatrists today provide only medications, not counseling. Nor are they as well trained in counseling as psychologists and licensed therapists are.
3. Psychologists and licensed therapists are educated and trained to provide counseling, and they may specialize in certain issues or populations. Some work in private counseling settings, while others work in public agencies where they can charge sliding-scale fees. The particular degree or license is not quite as important as the personality and the approach. I strongly believe that a therapist who is an open, honest, real human being, willing to self-disclose in an appropriate way, is much more helpful than a detached, theory-driven professional.
4. It is important for a therapist to give you support and encouragement for involvement in a twelve-step program or any other kind of support group in addition to the counseling, if that is what you need.
5. Decide whether you are looking for short-term problem solving or long-term help with patterns and personal growth—or a combination of both problem solving and personal growth. Make it clear to your therapist if you have a preference, but for many the motivation to work on life growth evolves over time as part of the therapeutic process.
6. Residential programs, such as Breakthrough at Caron,

exist; however, they are strongly suggested as an adjunct to ongoing therapy, and are best used to accelerate progress and not as a quick fix.

7. Whether in individual, couples, or group therapy, a positive, supportive approach is much more effective and is favored over a confrontational approach, which is rarely used today.
8. Active, directive therapy is preferred over a passive approach for the issues addressed in this book. In the beginning, you may need some specific guidance and suggestions, somewhat like what you'd get from a coach or a mentor. This should lessen with time and with your ability to direct your own process. Your goal should be to work hard in and out of the sessions and integrate what you learn into your life, not to sit and have it done to you.
9. Group therapy is very effective but sometimes hard to find. If you are in group therapy, you might also need to see a therapist outside the group on your own, either the group therapist or another therapist who is not involved in your group therapy sessions at all. Experiential therapy (also known as *action methods*), such as role-play or psychodrama, can sometimes be very helpful in getting unstuck. If your therapist does not do this kind of work, it may be wise to utilize a brief residential program such as Breakthrough at Caron or an ongoing therapy group that meets weekly and is facilitated by a therapist.
10. Couples therapy may be a necessary part of improving your quality of life. I strongly recommend therapists who are trained in emotionally focused couples therapy. An EFT therapist directory can be found at http://www.iceeft.com.

Another resource is the American Association of Marriage and Family Therapists (http://www.aamft.org) or *Psychology Today*'s Therapist Directory at http://www.therapist.psychology
today.com. Emotionally focused couples therapy is a process that has been proven to be successful and is often faster than other, more traditional methods. Don't settle for any therapist who isn't great at what he or she does.

11. Take responsibility for your own process. You are in counseling by choice as a consumer, and you have the right to leave at any time. You can decide when and how to take risks. When you believe your goals have been accomplished, therapy may be terminated. If you are not getting what you need in a reasonable amount of time (e.g., six months) or if you are not "clicking" with your therapist after a few weeks or months, move on and find someone else.

Summary

This chapter focused on the practices that help to improve quality of life—specifically, acceptance and humor. The paradox of acceptance is the key to happier relationships: the less you try to change others, the more they want to change. Tips were included on handling loved ones who do not want to change; dealing with someone else's perfectionism; finding role models for the courage to be yourself; building a strong support system; and finding the right guides, counselors, or therapists for your journey.

Chapter 8

Imperfect but Healthy Parenting—What Is a Healthy Family, Anyway?

There is nothing magical about creating a healthy family. We are born with every necessary tool to do it. Many of us, however, developed patterns in childhood that focused primarily on survival and maintaining minimal and inadequate connections with our parents rather than experiencing secure attachments. Once we reach a point where we are conscious of our needs, it is necessary for our approach to change as well. It isn't simply a matter of learning a better way. One's essence must be brought to the task, and we must be willing to take emotional risks, because secure attachment is the building block of healthy families.

The good news is that underneath all the pain and learned dysfunctional patterns, there lives a person who is full of love, has common sense, and wants to connect with others. It is reassuring to know that being healthy is much easier than trying to survive with old patterns.

There is no point in time at which we can certify a family as healthy. Most of us fluctuate between health and dysfunction as we are affected by changing conditions in our lives. The key really lies in being aware of the goal, what we are striving toward, and knowing we will never reach an actual finish line. There are way too many variables involved for us to expect to do it perfectly. When we are able to accept our own humanness and that of others, we can relax and enjoy the ride.

This message is clearly expressed at the end of the movie *Parenthood*, which I love, starring Steve Martin. When we ride on a roller coaster, we can keep our eyes open and embrace the excitement of it and the exhilaration of being alive, or we can close them and wait for it to be over while experiencing the least amount of distress possible. Which will you choose? I plan to enjoy the ride! Over the years I have been startled when my personal "roller coaster" nearly derailed a few times, but I'm still on it.

When we board the roller coaster at an amusement park, we assume that it has been thoroughly inspected for safety, and we make a conscious decision to trust it, despite what it looks like. Relationships are like this, too. It is up to the adults in the family to inspect and maintain the integrity of the system to be sure that it is safe for everyone. For this reason, I would like to address the issue of a healthy couple's relationship before discussing the family as a whole.

WHAT MAKES A COUPLE'S RELATIONSHIP HEALTHY?

When I wrote the first edition of this book, I was fairly young and not as experienced with this topic as I am now—at least not the successful parts. I was remarried shortly after the release of that edition.

Since then, I have had twenty years filled with a variety of all kinds of experience: some wanted, some I could have done without. All in all, my husband and I have learned to stick together and ride out the storms (mostly in regard to raising children). We have a great marriage in part because it was hard.

Relationships: You can't live with them, and you can't live without them. We are hardwired for attachment, and even when we say we don't need it, we go ahead and seek it anyway. Perfectionists want to take the risk out of relationships by controlling any uncertain factors. Unfortunately, this takes the fun out of relating. Intimacy can be pretty exciting and pretty terrifying all at the same time. Let's assume that you have worked through the pain with a process similar to what I described in Chapter 6. You may now be ready to take off your training wheels. You will not know how much you have grown until you take on the challenge of beginning or renewing a relationship.

Commitment

After dating and experiencing a lot of trial and error, you may finally settle on a person who seems right and then decide to commit to that person for life. The choice to commit is the most important step of all, if you know exactly what commitment means.

This is my personal definition: Commitment is a statement of my intention to remain constant in belief and action to a single ideal without entertaining other options, regardless of appearances, difficulties, or conflicts, which will arise in the pursuit of that ideal.

Commitment is not made through a marriage certificate or a verbal promise in front of clergy or a justice of the peace. We all know that a ceremony alone doesn't make a relationship work. The key to success is through the "one day at a time" vow you make to yourself that means you are entering the marriage or committed relationship with eyes wide open and with every intention of persevering. Your partner must make this vow as well. The vow must be made by two mature, informed, emotionally healthy (but imperfect) people who want the relationship to be healthy and thriving despite the challenges.

Commitment to something you know could fail is a paradox. Perfectionists are not very comfortable with paradoxes; they prefer certainty. Realistically, you know how hard it will be to keep your promise. You will have many moments when you want to quit. You also know that if you don't go into the relationship with positive intentions to work hard at it, you will surely fail. Commitment requires a leap of faith that is based in part on the knowledge of the strengths and weaknesses of yourself and your partner, not on a "love conquers all" approach.

Unfortunately, love has little to do with whether the relationship succeeds or fails. Love is also a choice, and it will need to be fostered and maintained. Love is created by the process of loving (the verb). You know it will get tough, and the two of you agree to remind each other about the commitment you have made during those tough times. Love can deepen and grow stronger from navigating the rapids of the tough times.

While you will be well aware of the possibility of failure, your chances for success will increase if you can understand and practice the rationale behind commitment. When you rule out the option of quitting or even threatening to quit, you make yourself vulnerable to being both hurt and loved by your partner. By fully committing, you make it safe for your partner to be real, open, and honest with you.

You and your partner don't stay together just because you vowed to, but you create a better relationship because of it. This is also a great foundation for building a healthy family system.

Interdependence

In an intimate relationship that lasts, there must be a certain amount of need for each other. Dependence means "I can't function without you" and "I am not whole unless you are there." Total independence means "I don't need you at all and would be just as happy without you." Some of both creates interdependence. As in most areas of life, aiming for a mixture or the middle is usually best.

With interdependence, the partners in a healthy relationship feel safe and supported. There is an agreement between the parties to be there for each other to the best of their abilities on a consistent basis. This does not imply perfection. Everyone has off days when he or she cannot be there for anyone. In an intimate, committed relationship, there is an understanding that the partners will be each other's best friend—but not each other's *only* friend. You might regularly seek the input or feedback of your partner but not rely on him or her to make your decisions or always agree.

Interdependence means that the partners can rely on each other without one assuming the problems, opinions, or feelings of the other. It is a tricky balance to learn to hold on to yourself while you give to another. In a dependent relationship, you would expect the other to suffer with you and fix you; then you wind up with two dysfunctional people instead of one. You can provide support and comfort to your partner and still have an emotional life of your own in an interdependent relationship.

Generally, in a healthy couple, the partners prefer to turn to each other first and then to family members or their friends. However, there will be times when you need more support from outside than from within your relationship. The two of you cannot expect to be all things to each other at all times. You each need your friends, family, or support group, in part so you don't wear each other out.

A boundary—such as "We will not turn to any person who could be a threat to our commitment and our life together"—may sometimes be needed with outside relationships, such as potential emotional affairs, friends who intrude, or family members who are not supportive of your relationship. This issue must be negotiated by the couple.

A perfectionist may occasionally have expectations like the following:

- "You should be there whenever I ask."
- "You should be on my side when I am upset with someone else."
- "If you loved me, you would change."

Implicit in interdependence is the understanding that human beings will not be capable of constant, perfect support. Resentment and hurt may result when you are needy and feel unsupported by your partner. Healthy people have enough self-worth and personal security to prevent them from feeling devastated or abandoned during times of fluctuation in a relationship. They express the hurt and move on. We each have a responsibility to take a personal inventory of our own positive and negative contributions to a relationship.

Emotional Intimacy

The primary difference between friendship and romantic attachment is the level of emotional intimacy. With commitment and an awareness of your essence, you are able to take bigger risks. You reveal more of who you are and trust your partner with vulnerabilities that others will never know. You hold the heart of another in your hands and trust him or her with the care of your heart. The process of being emotionally intimate takes time and attention in order to experience the rewards of committing to another human being fully. With care, an intimate relationship matures and evolves over the years. The care of a healthy relationship includes both partners doing the following:

- Taking individual responsibility for being present and available for each other. It is not always possible to do that, but it requires saving energy that you might spend on work, extended family, and even children. The house can even be an energy drainer that we must guard against.
- Setting aside regular time to spend together, away from children and friends. Your children will learn from your example.
- Sharing secrets, whether they are humorous stories or painful history. It means taking greater risks with each other than with anyone else.
- Having some space between you when it's needed: private interests, personal belongings, and physical space that is yours. It makes the coming together more meaningful.
- Having nonsexual contact that is spontaneous (not only ritual pecks on the cheek), including eye contact, touch, hugging, and lots of flirting.
- Wanting to know each other and help each other grow in whatever way your partner desires.
- Having fun with others together. This gives you a chance to know another aspect of your partner and brings balance to your expectations of the relationship.

A Growing and Changing Sexuality

Sexual intimacy grows with emotional intimacy. If you wish to have a healthy sexual relationship, you must also learn to enjoy and adjust to the changes and growth in your partners and yourself. Men and women are not the same. This is a basic fact that a healthy person with good self-esteem knows and enjoys. Partners in a gay relationship also understand and take pleasure in each other's uniqueness.

When you have a clear understanding of your essence, you feel more secure in developing a clear sexual identity. The person you are today is just that: the person you are today. Many variables affect how you relate sexually on any given day: physical well-being; stress; the frequency of intercourse; the level of intimacy in the relationship recently; unexpressed anger or resentment; worries about children, environment, or privacy; each partner's needs or expectations. This is not something you can control, predict, schedule, or do perfectly. The longer the two of you are together, the more affected you may be by these variables.

During the infatuation stage at the beginning of a relationship, you are blissfully blind and tend to tune out any distraction. This also changes with time. The beauty of a long-term relationship is the security and safety you feel once the intensity has lessened. You can take greater risks with a person you truly know and trust. The sexual relationship becomes an expression of intimacy rather than simply a physical exercise in mutual gratification. Intimacy precedes and follows good sex. Of course, it is possible to be satisfied occasionally without an emotional connection, but it does not contribute as much to the health of the relationship.

A healthy couple does not expect or need to be in sync with each encounter, but each partner takes pleasure in the pleasure of the other. It is interdependent: you both gain something and you both give something, but not necessarily at the same time or in equal proportions. You are each ultimately responsible for your own sexuality, conserving energy for sex, feeling attractive, and communicating needs and the changes in what you desire. You should not expect your partner to read your mind. As in any healthy communication, a healthy couple stays current with both partners' feelings.

Communication

Every couple says they wants to work on and improve communication. I'm convinced that what most people want is for their partner to be better at it. Most miscommunications begin with the tone or word choice of one partner, which then triggers a similar response from the other. You may feel shamed, put down, ignored, or disrespected. You would like the other person to change the way he or she talks and own up to the true meaning of that tone of voice. This type of conflict can go on forever unless you are able to get under it to what the unmet need is for each individual.

Here is an example of a recurring interaction described in one couple's session: Jillian and Karen have been married for about two years but have lived together for seven. They both have stressful jobs, despite the fact that Karen works out of their home, which is currently under construction. Jillian usually arrives home around 6:00 PM.

The previous weekend they had entertained Karen's family: her sister and her two young children—a real handful for them, since their usable space is limited. The guests didn't leave until Sunday evening. On Monday, Karen and Jillian got up early, and Jillian had to rush out without saying goodbye. Karen knew that she had to catch up on paperwork since she spent Friday getting ready for their guests. By 3:00 PM she was exhausted from working nonstop. In the back of her mind, she was hoping that Jillian would be able to help her clean up the house when she got home.

Jillian was glad to be at work today and out of the house. She had been generous with her time and patient through the entire weekend of chaos, but in all honesty, she couldn't stand her niece and her nephew. She didn't complain, and she was upbeat for Karen's benefit. Jillian was sure that Karen would be appreciative of all she did for her family. Driving home that evening, Jillian wondered if there might be a nice dinner and a foot rub waiting as a reward. She arrived home a little late and was met at the door by Karen, who appeared disheveled and tired, with obviously little or no effort put into her appearance.

"You're late!" Karen exclaimed. "Was the traffic bad?"

Jillian, puzzled by the question, asked, "Why, did something happen here?"

"Not really," Karen replied. "I just thought you might try to get home earlier."

"Why would I?" Jillian wanted to know.

Karen, frustrated by Jillian's lack of awareness, retorted, "The house is a mess, can't you see it?"

"I guess it is," Jillian admitted. "Didn't you have time to clean up?"

In her defense, Karen snapped back, "I thought you would help me! I guess that's not going to happen now." Huffing and puffing, she began to clean.

Jillian countered sarcastically, "Do you think I didn't do enough for you already?" She went out on the deck and sat down. As the two distanced themselves from each other, both felt misunderstood and unappreciated.

This type of argument would usually end with days of silence, leaving both feeling abandoned and unable to process what had happened. They blamed each other and pondered over the details of the problem to figure out who was at fault.

Does this type of communication sound familiar? What happened here was partly predictable yet challenging to analyze. The expectations left unexpressed by both may be obvious to you. Also, notice the indirect anger and sarcasm. This suggests that the topics of Karen's family and the issue of "Who does more?" (i.e., who handles more responsibility at home and at work) might be perpetual problems.

As a therapist, I could rewrite their dialogue and put in all the right words for each person to say, but research has shown that a couple is not able to sustain "perfect" communication for very long when emotions are running high. A more effective approach is to analyze the interaction in order to learn the attachment needs hidden beneath the expectations. What do you suppose each was looking for or needing from the other? The following shows the real needs underlying most communication—many of the needs we are unaware of when we are grouchy or upset in our closest relationships:

- Closeness and distance
- Feeling valued and important
- Appreciation and recognition
- Respect for one's thoughts and feelings
- Sexual contact and expression
- Support for one's dreams
- Acceptance
- Reassurance of love and commitment

During their next therapy session, Karen and Jillian determined and described their needs and behaviors during that argument.

Karen, a self-described perfectionist, was feeling stressed and anxious. In the session, she told Jillian that she wasn't ready to talk when Jillian got home that night. She laughed now, remembering how she had believed that her primary need on Monday night was for Jillian to help her clean the house. That evening, in the back of her mind, she had been very disappointed and sad about how her sister had handled her children during the visit. It made her think of her own childhood, which was very painful. Karen admitted that she wanted to work out her frustration rather than talk about it.

Karen's pattern had always been to work out her feelings alone. She did this by trying to bring order to her surroundings. Karen wanted Jillian's company while she was upset, but she hadn't been able to share her pain yet. She needed distance from her problems first and for Jillian to just be there for her. She acknowledged that she might have wanted to talk later, after they had cleaned the house.

Jillian listened and was surprised by the level of Karen's pain and the method she had used to deal with the circumstances that had caused it. She was also relieved to hear that Karen cares about her and that she wants her nearby when she is trying to work through difficult, painful issues. Jillian hadn't known this until now.

After Karen's disclosure, Jillian said that she had also been stressed by the weekend, but in a different way. She felt drained and emotionally needy. She had hoped that Karen would soothe her and express gratitude, which Jillian later realized was a little premature. She too felt resentful of Karen's sister and the children's bad behavior, but sensing Karen's pain, she had been afraid to bring it up. Selfishly, she had just wanted to be heard and possibly validated in her own concerns. Now she understood that Karen hadn't been ready to do that but was willing now.

After they had shared their real needs, it was possible for them to "lean toward" each other. Success with this type of communication depends on self-awareness and a willingness to listen with empathy. It is a skill that must be developed through determination and practice, but one person cannot do it alone. It is still okay to argue and work your way back to a deeper dialogue. The original problem often dissolves in the process.

Within the relationship, time and setting will often influence the quality of communication. For example, you may think that the time spent driving to work and back is a good opportunity to share. The car, unfortunately, is a very poor setting. You cannot have eye contact or observe body language to enhance your understanding of your partner. It takes work to make the time for such an important interaction.

Daily opportunities for sharing feelings about responsibilities, career issues, and children are needed. Private opportunities—when not exhausted—to talk about more intimate subjects such as sex, feelings about each other, and so on are needed as well. Staying current prevents the buildup of resentments and pain from misunderstandings.

Listening is a much-neglected area of communication. When afraid or threatened, there is a tendency to block what you hear in order to prepare a defense. Listening requires total availability, visual and physical. Since relationships frequently fail because of poor communication, this needs to be kept a priority. If a strong foundation exists in your relationship, it will be easier to have a healthy family.

WHAT MAKES A FAMILY HEALTHY?

Clients, workshop attendees, and professionals all over the country frequently ask me what makes a family healthy. I often reply by asking them to tell me what *they* think makes a family healthy. This section summarizes their responses and the effective approaches of many parents and families. Keep in mind that the philosophies and behaviors discussed below are ideals to aim for, not goals to achieve. There is no room for perfectionism when children and stepchildren are involved.

Parenting Is a Priority

Ideally, adults who choose to be parents do so knowing the responsibility they are assuming. They develop a balance between having their lives as adults and putting their children ahead of many other things that would be important if they were not parents. Parenting means sacrifice by choice, not as a victim.

Parenting means realizing when you don't know what you are doing and seeking help or information. It means acknowledging the limitations caused by your own family background. It means sharing fully this task with the child's other parent, if possible, and, in some cases, putting aside negative feelings for that parent for the benefit of the child. As a single parent, you may be required to keep some things to yourself about your ex (the child's mom or dad), letting the child discover what is real for him or herself.

Parenting requires playing when you don't really want to, putting your exhaustion and heartaches aside for the benefit of the child, knowing your child, and being sensitive to unverbalized needs. A healthy parent talks to a child who has become quiet or anxious to find out what's going on inside.

As a parent, you get to reexperience childhood. This may trigger both painful and happy memories. At times, emotional needs will need to be postponed until the children are asleep or away from you—then you can let the tears flow. It can be a selfless job, with periods of little reward. You may not have the time or the privacy to talk to friends on the phone, go to your favorite restaurant, or watch a movie, because it isn't best for the children. You may have to wait to make time for your personal needs or desires because the needs of your children are constant and unpredictable.

You will need to slow down to see the beauty of your children and feel the immense love you give and receive, because there is no guarantee of getting anything back. They will not know what you did for them until they are parents, and maybe not even then. Yet to all of this we make a lifetime commitment and can't imagine life without it!

Feelings Are Appropriately Expressed

The healthy expression of feelings within a family requires that the parents know their own feelings and develop healthy ways of managing and sharing them as needed. The conversation that follows is an example of the safe communication of feelings.

At the dinner table, Mom confides to her family, "I'm a little sad today. My friend at work left for a new job."

Dad replies sympathetically, "I'm sorry. I'm sure you will miss her."

Their six-year-old child says, "My teacher is mean."

"How was she mean?" Dad asks.

The child replies, "She didn't pick me for leader at recess."

"Did that hurt your feelings?" Dad probes.

"Yes, and I was really mad at her," the child confirms.

Dad asks, perceptively, "What did you do with your mad feeling?"

"I told my friend," replies the child.

Dad positively responds, "That was a good choice. Good for you!"

Listening to the feelings of your partner and your children is a great way to model. Children see how it's done and imitate. Parents may guide their children by setting limits and teaching new skills as needed, but they should at least try to integrate the concepts themselves before they preach them to their children. Many adults may need to seek additional help through reading books, attending support groups, and researching tips and guidance for these skills. The process of attaining these skills must start with dealing with your own feelings.

The boundaries and limits set by parents around emotional expression protect not only the child but also the adults from the harm of attachment injuries. In healthy families, children know what the limits are. Here are two examples of limits set by the single mother of a twelve-year-old girl: "You may be angry with me, but you may not say, 'I hate you.'" "It is not okay to hit anyone, throw things, or destroy property."

The specific limits in each home will be unique, determined by the values of the parents and the needs of the children. Respect, kindness, and honesty should be expected even when someone is upset.

When children share painful feelings—fear, loneliness, or hurt—healthy parents manage their own anxiety and do not overreact, nor do they shame or minimize. They accept the feelings as normal and listen, resulting in the following:

- Tears and sadness are allowed and are considered healthy.
- There is no need to fix a problem immediately, but when consistent patterns appear, the parents will attempt to find the cause and correct the problem or get help, if necessary.

- Professional help is seen as a useful tool whenever the family is stuck or needs extra support.
- The parents inform the children in an age-appropriate way that something is wrong. They neither depend on their children nor pretend that nothing is wrong. For example, a father who has just lost his job knows that telling his children what happened is very important but that reassuring them that he knows what to do about it is also important.

Children worry and are afraid when they see their parents struggling. Healthy parents can take care of themselves while also attending to the needs of their children. In this way, parents can model to their children that talking helps, that no one has to do it alone, and that problems can be solved in time.

There Are Visible Signs of Health

The healthy family does not have to look good in the social sense, with the best clothes or perfect behavior, but there will be observable signs of the good feelings in a family, such as the following:

- The family members make eye contact, looking directly at one another when they talk.
- Smiles will not be constant, but you will sense that these people like one another.
- Touch, in the form of gentle and appropriate physical contact, and relaxed postures make the family members look comfortable.
- Humor and laughter (not teasing and sarcasm) are evident at times, demonstrating a positive outlook and a shared humorous view of the world.

- Openness and comfort with one another are demonstrated through attentive listening or even comfort with silence.
- Conflict is handled without defensiveness or blame.

Every family goes through bad times when communication shuts down or the individuals don't feel as safe as usual. This must be seen as a dynamic process, not a fixed way of being. In family therapy, it becomes clear in a moment whether the healthy factors above are present. Even when a healthy family is in crisis, some of those factors will remain. What shines through it all is their love for one another, both felt and expressed.

There Is a Proactive Approach to Stress

Since a crisis is not necessary for distraction in a healthy family, it is not well tolerated. Parents model for their children how to foresee a problem coming and how to prevent it, if possible. They demonstrate the importance of planning, researching alternatives, seeking necessary information, and learning how to disagree and negotiate in an attempt to solve what can be solved.

Healthy parents believe that although life has its difficulties, it is not a constant struggle. The parents are able to see past the crisis. They continue to live and attend to important things, like parenting, while they address the problem.

In a healthy marriage, the couple is able to work together in a crisis. The partners may disagree about the solution, but they will share the goal of resolution. They will not use the crisis as an excuse to blame each other or to distract from other, more serious problems. When life has been chaotic or stressful, the parents restore order by returning to routine, structure, and predictability. Children feel secure knowing that someone is in charge and is taking control of the situation.

Stress can also be caused by too much of a good thing. Parents who take children to lessons and sports activities every evening may find that the core of the family is weakening. Everyone needs structured family time in order to have intimacy and opportunities to communicate. A busy family can be a very stressed-out family.

Moderation and balance are reflected in both the positive and the negative aspects of a healthy family. I envision the model healthy family system as a cross between television's current-day *Modern Family*, which premiered in 2009, and *The Cosby Show*, which aired in the 1980s and early 1990s. I have to admit, however, that in TV sitcoms, moderation just isn't considered funny; extremes are the norm.

What makes these families great are their flexibility, humor, individuality, approaches to conflict, and risk taking. The family members have different ways of doing things and inevitably have clashing opinions, yet they are supported and encouraged to be authentic. I also appreciate that no individual and neither sex is scapegoated. All characters' flaws or mistakes are highlighted equally. They talk, they worry, they feel, but most important, they love and accept one another for whomever they are, all in under thirty minutes.

Since they feel secure and relaxed, the members of a healthy family are able to grow and change as they learn new things, and they are encouraged to take risks. This behavior is modeled by the parents for their children and encouraged as a way of life.

Disagreements and Differences of Opinion Occur

When individuals in a family have strong personal identities, they will frequently clash. The same will happen when the children grow up and go out into the world as adults. Family is the learning lab for life. The best place to witness and experience conflict effectively is at home. Parents who are real and open are the best role models. Not only will they have conflicts with each other, but life also gives them many opportunities to face people outside the family with anger and different opinions. A healthy family is not necessarily a quiet one. It is okay to fight, but the skills of fair fighting are taught.

The Family System Is Open to Outside Support

A healthy family is an open, dynamic system, growing and changing with time. A support system exists for each individual in the family in the form of friends or school groups. Religious communities, recovery groups, neighbors, extended family members (grandparents, aunts, uncles, and cousins), and old family friends all serve as support for the health of the family as a whole. People will come and go, and the children may have preferences and dislike some, but an important life lesson is the overall security that comes from knowing we are not alone.

Sometimes home does not feel like a safe place. At those times, an established support system may carry the family through. During periods of financial stress, health problems, or tragedy, this support system may truly hold up the family. People who do not have extended family support need to develop this type of support from their community. No family is an island.

Parenting Means Guiding and Letting Go

In healthy families, there is an understanding that parenting is a gradual, continuous process of letting go of children from birth to adulthood. Initially, parents are totally responsible for their children, but later they serve only as occasional guides. It is the duty of parents to protect children while they grow into the beautiful people they are supposed to be. Healthy parents have hopes for their children but do not have an agenda of expectations for them. "Perfect" parenting would assume that parents know exactly what their children need.

Discipline is aimed at protecting the child, not at making the parent more comfortable. It addresses the behavior, not the worth, of the child. It uses natural or logical consequences so that the child learns to self-correct rather than to look to others for approval or disapproval.

Using punishment inevitably creates a battle of wills between the parent and the child. Healthy discipline becomes the means by which a child learns what works best for him or her to get the desired results in life. Children develop internal motivation to make good choices and learn from their mistakes. Parents approach their children with the confidence that they will be successful with practice, and they are prepared to intervene when a lack of readiness is evident.

In a healthy family, children are respected for being able to say no. Parents may have concerns about what their children say no to, but overall it is a good skill to have. Saying no to a blue shirt today may eventually help with saying no to marijuana or alcohol. The parent who can support the process while addressing areas of disagreement one at a time will have a healthier child. Many times, saying no is really the child's need to say to a parent, "I am *me,* I am not you!" Parents who are secure themselves and have a strong identity view this as a positive skill.

Limit setting is the responsibility of healthy parents. Limits are like an invisible shield around children, protecting them until they are ready to stretch further. A two-year-old needs a very small space to operate in, and a fifteen-year-old needs a very big space. But neither has the ability to handle total freedom in the world. Healthy discipline provides this limit in the form of family rules and structure, not in the form of punishment. Instead of punishment, there are consequences that make sense and that fit the mistake.

Children are supposed to make lots of mistakes. The more they make while they are children, the fewer they will need to make as adults. Experience is growth.

Affirmation and Praise Work Together

Praise, which we addressed briefly in Chapter 6, is a nice way to motivate children and adults to succeed. It is important in the development of achievers: children who get good grades and who seek excellence in what they do. Healthy families balance praise with affirming the worth and value of the person. It is more important for children to feel good about themselves and know that they are loved than to have their parents applaud their accomplishments. When parents take great *personal* pride in the good things their children do, this may be perceived as pressure to please the parents rather than encouragement of the children to find pleasure and pride in the achievements for themselves.

A healthy family incorporates affirmation and praise into everyday living as naturally as breathing. Living with affirmation creates positive self-talk in adults and children. Family members have more positive than negative self-talk, and the children grow up able to pass it on to their own children.

A Perfectionist Child Receives Guidance

If a child is born with the tendency for perfectionism, it will be fairly obvious by the time he or she is three years old. It won't be a problem as long as the parents are able to provide balance and guidance as the child grows and enters school. With any trait that could become a problem, the parents will need to accept the child's temperament as it is and offer suggestions and tools throughout the child's development. If one of the parents is also a perfectionist, it may be easier if he or she has done some work on self-acceptance and letting go.

Having grown up in a Catholic school, Theresa knew how to be a good girl and was praised for her perfect attendance and homework through elementary school and beyond. She remembered the pressure she felt and how she cried as she did her homework over and over until it was right. She was never satisfied, and no one knew how to help her.

Now that she was a mother herself and aware of the issue, she wanted to help her "perfect" five-year-old daughter, Marcy, to lighten up and not strive for perfection the way she had. Her son, who was three, didn't seem to have an issue with trying too hard the way Marcy did. She read about child development and spoke to her therapist about what to do for Marcy.

The first thing Theresa realized was that she was being too hard on herself as a parent. She had to learn to relax and understand that she was already a better parent than her own mother or father had been and that Marcy was already loved unconditionally. The rest was not very difficult.

Theresa and her husband were able to affirm Marcy as a person and praise her when she was having fun and when she worked hard. They allowed some flexibility with both children in the way they managed their rooms. Theresa decided that her husband was more fun for reading stories at night because he didn't push Marcy to read right away. When it appeared that Marcy was pushing herself or was easily frustrated with a new task, Theresa and her husband would break it down into small steps and give Marcy some encouragement to just take the first step.

They taught by example in their daily activities, using phrases like "That's enough for now," "I don't have to be a perfect reader," or "We don't have to hurry." They also concentrated on the balance of work and play as a family. Through the years their approach would have to be adjusted, but they were on the right track.

If Divorce Occurs, It Is Done in a Healthy Way

Divorce or separation can occur even within a healthy family. This too can be done with health, although it will not be without pain. Respect, if not love, can be maintained between the parents so that a healthy parenting relationship may continue. Divorce in and of itself does not damage children. The way we live before and during the divorce may, however. Healthy couples have a choice about how they go about getting divorced. This is not an easy task, and it will not be done perfectly.

The Parents Are Open About Family History

The children in a healthy family will know where they came from—the good and the bad. The parents will share what they know about the family history—if possible, recording information and pictures that tell the story. Most important, there will be no secrets. Children will be told in age-appropriate doses about painful events in the lives of their parents and their grandparents along with the family stories that are humorous and interesting.

Information about mental illness, alcoholism, adoption, death, and divorce has less emotional charge when shared at an early age with children in a language they understand. It is only when they believe it has been withheld, or if they sense the parents' pain about it, that they will be disturbed.

For example, a mother who is an incest survivor may calmly share the following information with her three-year-old: "Your body is your own; no one should touch you without your permission. Once when I was little, I was touched in a way I didn't like, but I didn't know I could say no. I didn't tell my mother, and that hurt me very much. I want you to say no, and you can tell me if anyone ever tries to hurt you, no matter what he or she says."

As the child matures, the information can be made more specific. Healthy parents want to prevent future pain for their children by being honest and open today.

Single Parents Model Intimacy

A healthy relationship between the divorced or separated parents is just as important to the children as it is to the couple. Children can learn how to have healthy relationships only from watching the adults around them.

In a single-parent family, this modeling must be done through friendships or serious dating relationships. It is important for children in a single-parent situation to spend time around healthy couples. The single parent can also model what it is like to be alone by choice in a healthy way, which teaches another important skill.

In a healthy family, the children witness the specialness of adult relationships and come to expect similar healthy bonds when they grow up. They will come to know the difference between sexual attraction and love. They will know when they are being treated poorly, because they have been raised with respect and kindness.

Children with high self-esteem can begin to choose their friends based on the feelings they have about themselves. This is the beginning of learning to have healthy relationships.

Summary

A healthy family starts with healthy adult relationships with yourself and others. When love is the center of a family, home becomes the haven it was intended to be. It can be the safest place there is, where you know you can be yourself and still be loved. A family also needs a village to thrive in and to give support during hard times.

Beginning with your imperfect, authentic self is the only way to get closer to this ideal. You cannot give your children what you were never given and therefore don't have. Simply creating a looking-good family is not the answer. With effort, you may be able to pay it forward by changing your family for generations to come. Every step you take is important.

Chapter 9

Finding Balance in Imperfection

This chapter is about balance, an elusive state of being that can be achieved only by the imperfect. The chapter includes options to bring fun into your life whenever you need it, tips for staying in balance, and some much-needed spirituality. It also deals with the question "Am I there yet?" If you are still committed to remaining a perfectionist, you will be tempted to deem this chapter too frivolous and lacking in enough intensity to keep your interest. Please read on, however.

IMPERFECT THINGS TO DO AND ENJOY

Over the years, I have brought balance into my life by consciously hiring people who have a great sense of humor and are comfortable taking risks, some of which bordered on the bizarre much of the time. I asked this fun-loving group to assist in the preparation of the list below. As a perfectionist, you will probably need such a source to reference, since you tend to have difficulty coming up with creative, fun ideas on your own. The list is broken down into activities you can perform with a friend, a willing partner, or by yourself. Take what's useful and share the rest with your friends.

Things to Do with a Friend or a Partner

- Take a walk on a rainy day, stepping in puddles along the way.
- Play old music and dance without worrying about how you look.
- Get the funniest movie you've ever seen and invite friends over for popcorn and laughs. (Don't clean the house first.)
- Watch children's movies or read children's books. You are making up for lost time here.
- Play crazy games for laughs, not competition. Larger gatherings are fun for this.
- Share ridiculous jokes or stories.

Twelve Imperfect Activities to Do by Yourself

- Keep wind-up toys in your office and play with them.
- Set the alarm on your phone for a "breathing break" several times a day. Stand up and take a few deep breaths or do something else you enjoy for a minute.
- Keep a jar at home full of nurturing, fun things you love to do on little slips of paper. Examples: taking a bubble bath, shooting hoops, riding your bike, playing jacks, reading, listening to music, and dancing. Pick one whenever you're feeling needy or low, and definitely include these on your weekly chore to-do list.
- Post specific affirmations you may need where you will see them regularly and easily: on the bathroom mirror, in the

kitchen cupboard, on the refrigerator door, and in the car. Move them and change them often so they stay relevant and visible to you. Examples: "You have done enough." "You are important." "I accept myself as I am today." "Today, something wonderful is going to happen." "You are good enough." "Choose love."

- Deliberately leave something undone every day. At the end of the day, reflect on it and tell someone proudly that you were able to let go.
- On Saturday (or whatever day is chore day for you), make a list of things you have no intention of doing and *don't do them*!
- Be very quiet several times a day, especially when you are too busy. Answers will come; priorities will become clear.
- Simplify. This means gradually cleaning your attic and getting rid of the clutter in your life. The less you have, the less you need to keep track of. It also means don't buy what you don't need. Hire others to do things you don't like to do. You'd be amazed at how inexpensive housekeeping is and how good you feel when you aren't doing it all. It can also mean settling for less than excellence in things that don't matter, leaving more energy for what does.
- Stop your work and build fun into your day. Even while writing this book, I planned to do something distracting in the middle of each day whenever I needed it: a puzzle to work on, music to listen to, a friend to have lunch with.
- When you feel especially stressed, let go and do nothing. There are times when less is more. Instead of taking control and trying to do more to resolve the problem, breathe, meditate, take a walk, do something else, or simply do nothing. The

problem may solve itself, someone else will handle it, or an answer will come to you.

- Avoid extremes. Even good things can be taken too far: recovery, exercise, healthy eating, and even fun. Being real and spontaneous does not have to mean reverting to your inner child. Balance leaves you open to a variety of opportunities, and you can spontaneously choose among those you like best. You will also occasionally lose it and become compulsive. That's okay, too.
- Seek out children. Parents and grandparents of young children have a built-in balancer; others will need to borrow children from a friend. Kids have the best ideas for fun. Spending fun time with children can be a choice rather than a duty or an obligation. Adults can have a lot of fun if they choose the best time for play and don't depend solely on children's choices. Include things that you like to do as well.

AFFIRMATIONS FOR THE AVERAGE: A MEDITATION

One final suggestion to assist in your enjoyment of imperfection is to listen to the following meditation each day or whenever you need a reminder of how perfect you are right now. I was inspired to write this meditation for myself many years ago after reading Shakti Gawain's book *Living in the Light: A Guide to Personal and Planetary Transformation.*[1]

I would recommend that you record this, or your own version of it, in your own voice so that you can listen to it regularly.

1 Shakti Gawain, *Living in the Light: A Guide to Personal and Planetary Transformation* (San Raphel, CA: Whatever Publishing, 1991).

Relax your body and your mind in whatever way is most comfortable for you. Become conscious of your breathing, letting go of distractions, concerns, and tension. Let worries and to-do lists float away with every breath.

Prepare to listen carefully to the new, more positive belief system that is growing within you.

In each of us, there is a natural ability and a willingness to learn new things. For this moment, you have no need or desire to resist. You feel very open to a new understanding of yourself and others.

The critical voices of your parents, those in authority, and your own mental "committee" are silent for now.

With each breath, in each moment, you can choose to believe these new positive messages.

A new voice of love and acceptance is developing in you that will soon silence any critical thoughts.

Your essence is seeking the safety, acceptance, and unconditional love that this voice will provide. Listen now to this new affirming voice:

- I honor and celebrate my humanness.
- My only responsibility is to be true to myself—to embrace my essence. There is no need to be perfect or to act perfectly.
- My greatest assets are my honesty, spontaneity, and willingness to risk.
- I can enjoy being still. I am supposed to make mistakes—I was made that way.
- My humanness makes it easier for others to love me and reach out to me.
- What I'm doing is just enough.

- My body is healthy and perfect just the way it is.
- I can trust my inner voice to tell me what I need. I am lovable no matter what I do.
- I accept myself exactly as I am, for today, this moment.

Pause now and breathe in what you have heard with your hand on your heart.

[If recording, stop here.]

TIPS FOR PROCRASTINATORS

In light of the fact that I am not a full-time procrastinator, I've put this section off long enough. Perfectionists have a special way of procrastinating that differs from other types of procrastinators, so I would like to address that kind only, since it is my area of expertise. For information and research on all types of procrastinators and the issue in general, I suggest additional reading, starting with *The Now Habit* by Neil Fiore.[2]

I like his approach, and I suggest you read his book in its entirety, using it as a workbook if you truly want to change your particular pattern.

The following tips are for those perfectionists who are also procrastinators:

1. If you are a covert perfectionist, take a moment the next time you are facing a task you would normally avoid. Write or type any and all negative thoughts that come up about the task and your ability to do it. Take as long as you need to get

2 Neil A. Fiore, *The Now Habit: A Strategic Program for Overcoming Procrastination and Enjoying Guilt-Free Play* (New York: Penguin, 2007).

them on paper, then put them aside. They are just thoughts, and they must be allowed to come and go. The negative thoughts don't get to make decisions about your day. This can be repeated every time you start to work on a task.

2. If you are an overt perfectionist, take a moment to set up your space so that you cannot see any other task that might need to be done. Better yet, do that the day before you plan to start a task. You need a clear view to have a clear head. If negative thoughts arise, review the previous step.
3. Whether you're an overt or a covert perfectionist, you should have a meditation book or reading of your choice ready in front of you. It must be one that speaks to you and calms you down easily. It has to make sense to you and speak to your anxiety. My choice today was *Illuminata* by Marianne Williamson. As I sat down to write this chapter, an overwhelming sensation and sheer panic ran through me. The following excerpt from the book spoke to me: "Dear God, I dedicate this work to You. Imprint Your mind upon it. Fly with it unto the heavens. Use it to shower Your love onto the world. Thank you for Your faith in me that such a glorious mission has been placed in my hands."[3]

It worked for me, but I have had a lot of practice using similar tools. It gets easier with time. I respond well to spiritual approaches, but if that is not your thing, find what is. Everyone has some anxiety when starting a large task, and I know that I have to address that first; otherwise, I go nowhere fast. You will need tools at your fingertips every day.

---

3 Marianne Williamson, *Illuminata: Thoughts, Prayers, Rites of Passage* (New York: Random House, 1994), p. 192.

4. If this is a medium-size task that will take more than one day, split it into parts. Write down your plan for today first and then each day backward from the deadline, if there is one. The hardest parts should be allocated more time. Each day *must* end with something simple and fun that is preplanned—a reward for sticking with it even if you didn't do everything you planned: a long shower, a foot massage, or time on the deck. Don't skip the fun, no matter what.
5. This schedule is a guide for your time, not a mandate, and it must be manageable. If you do more or less than you planned, make changes to the dates and times on the schedule. Set a specific block of time, and if you finish early, stop and do something fun.
6. Listen to the Affirmations for the Average meditation above and thank yourself for taking a step in the right direction by facing your fear and putting negative thoughts and self-doubt aside.
7. Commit to the process in these steps rather than saying, "From now on . . . ," which never works. The process is not a task, it is a way of approaching tasks, and thus it is flexible. Yet it can become a permanent way of doing things, if it works for you.

"AM I THERE YET?": KNOWING WHEN YOU ARE HEALTHY

Since the goal is not perfection and you will never truly arrive at such a point, how do you know when you are well enough to call yourself *healthy*? For the most part, I believe it is when you have achieved inner strength, security, stability, and an awareness that you are okay. There are, however, some specific guideposts, which many people who are committed to growth (I like to call them *seekers*) have shared and demonstrated throughout their experiences. These are described below.

You Have Incorporated Spiritual Practices into Daily Living

Being spiritual does not mean being perfect and godlike. You can have a very healthy, spiritual life and make lots of mistakes. Healthy spirituality is a conscious awareness of your human limitations and an openness to influence from inside yourself and from outside through others. Something inside speaks to you through your essence, your instincts, and your sense of what is right. When you are healthy, you seek that inner guidance as easily as you breathe. It is not something you do at a particular time of the day, although that may be part of your expression of spirituality. It is something that is part of everything you do.

When faced with a struggle, a decision, a problem, or a conflict, the first thing you do is reflect, pray, and look inward or upward, whichever seems right. You no longer strive for control through your intellect. In health, you realize that letting go and reaching out brings more security than trying harder to do more. At times, the answer may be to simply live with the problem as it is for now. When you feel joy or success, there is an appreciation that you are in partnership with something higher than just your own resources. You are not alone on the good days or the bad.

Healthy spirituality may be expressed through organized religion without the expectation that the institution, composed of imperfect people, will be perfect. You do not rigidly adhere to rules without first sifting information through your own beliefs and values. Sometimes you will disagree with what a particular person or religious authority believes to be true. It is not an all-or-nothing matter. You can be an active member of a religious group without accepting all of its beliefs.

I believe that eventually the spiritual person will feel a need to share his or her spirituality with others through some group experience. Many twelve-step groups have served such a purpose for recovering people. Others will find an ongoing support system or family in which they may openly express this essential part of themselves. Without such expression, there may be isolation and doubt. Spirituality grows in numbers, and you will occasionally need to be reminded by others to look for answers from a higher consciousness. The group serves this purpose.

A healthy person can be recognized in a crisis as the one who is still centered and at peace. Although you have your ups and downs, there is a higher belief that you are being cared for and that there is meaning and growth in every experience. You know you will be okay no matter what the outcome.

You have developed your own prescription for peace that does not involve unnecessary drugs. (Some individuals may continue to struggle with clinical depression, anxiety, or other mood disorders that may require ongoing medication. That does not mean they are emotionally unhealthy.) A prescription for peace is made up of the people, places, and things you turn to again and again that bring you back to center. My personal plan includes reading; listening at length to speakers who inspire me; reading books that inspire me; praying; turning to nature; spending time and talking with my family and those I love, including my children and grandchildren; and making a conscious effort to express gratitude for all the love in my life and all that I have experienced. My tools are not out of reach. I need them frequently. I use them almost daily. I advise you to write your own prescription.

You Feel What You Feel

When you are healthy, there is no sense of urgency to get rid of the feelings you experience. You are comfortable with being angry, afraid, sad, or loving. You allow feelings to come and go, without judgment or shame, taking responsibility for your own response to the world. No one causes you to feel or react in a particular way, nor does anyone have to change to make your bad feelings go away.

When you are angry, you may choose to share it with someone outside the situation before approaching the source. You are aware that you are not thinking clearly through the anger and do not want to make serious mistakes. When you are sad, you may simply cry or take time to be alone with the feeling before trying to relieve yourself of it by sharing.

You allow friends and family to see you when your feelings are unattractive, but you also are able to use discretion, choosing when not to express yourself (e.g., at work). You are able to postpone expression of pain for the needs of the situation or the protection of others, such as children, knowing you will get back to it as soon as you can. You then address it by feeling it, talking to someone in your support system, or just letting it out.

Feelings are not your enemy. They are a personal compass: a special, unique, and dynamic part of your essence, which you use to guide yourself and to connect with those who share in your life.

You are also tolerant of the feelings of others, seeing them as ever changing, allowing those you love to be responsible for themselves. Although you may never enjoy being around pain, you are willing to listen for the benefit of another and for the growth of the relationship.

You Feel Choice (Not Power) over Compulsive Behavior

You are healthy when you are no longer driven or obsessed with things. Occasionally, you will use compulsiveness to cope. The difference is that you know exactly what you are doing, and you are prepared to suffer the consequences without blaming anyone else. You also believe that whether you use food, work, shopping, or something else, you eventually will have to deal with the feelings behind it and the consequences. No one is expected to do it for you. It is not about circumstances forcing you to do it. You are a victim to no one but your own choices.

If some aspect of your life becomes unmanageable, you seek appropriate help and take action. Living in pain is no longer acceptable. I recently received a letter from a former client who has been struggling for years with her nicotine dependence. She had become well enough to quit and wrote, "I've had some difficulty finding the right kind of help, so I set up a sort of outpatient program for myself, with different therapies, bodywork, and a new health and diet regimen. It seems like my world has changed—it has inside, anyway. This certainly is the biggest event of my recovery."

It is normal to continue to have some struggles in your life. It is healthy to approach them with choice, a sense of responsibility, and hope for progress. When you are healthy, you believe that nothing is beyond your ability to improve. You then choose if and when to work on it and whom to enlist in support of your mission.

You Are Physically Healthy Most of the Time

No one will ever perfect the human body, but a healthy person does not welcome the stress that contributes to illness. You care about your body and try to provide the best possible surroundings for your physical and emotional growth. Self-care involves consciousness of what you ingest, of your need for exercise, of potential medical problems, and of what you need to do for yourself. It does not involve doing it all perfectly.

In this world it requires great effort to maintain balance between the extremist messages of "you must be perfect" and "the environment is going to kill you anyway." Listening to your body and its messages to you in each moment helps to make you aware of what you need. Sometimes you choose to listen and sometimes you ignore it, but whatever you do, you are making a conscious choice.

Emotionally healthy people are likely to have fewer illnesses, since positive living is known to affect immunity. This is not to say you'll have a problem-free life, but you'll have an outlook of hope and a willingness to feel what you feel. Without self-induced emotional stress and negativity, you are able to fight off illness, and with close relationships and support, healing is possible.

You Stretch Yourself Beyond Who You Are Today

Intellectual growth is an ongoing process of seeking. As a healthy person, you accept yourself, but you also desire to learn more, simply for the joy of doing it. If you have discovered your essence, this may mean looking for a new career that is a better fit, going back to school, seeking a promotion, traveling, finding a mentor, or studying something new. You are never finished learning.

You are comfortable, though challenged, around those who know more than you do, because you are also aware that you have strengths in other areas. You are comfortable in being the student, and you try to bring people into your life with the knowledge or experience that will help you to evolve beyond your present limitations.

You Have a Solid, Stable Family of Choice and a Positive Relationship with Your Family of Origin

Healthy people take responsibility for getting their needs met and have developed a network of support in their lives. This might include a best friend, a spouse or lover, a sister, a fellow twelve-step group member, a coworker, or a mentor. You probably will not share everything with everyone and may not even see those in your support system frequently. You realize that attempting to manage intimate relationships with a large number of people can be an overwhelming challenge, so instead you choose to focus on the quality of a smaller number of meaningful relationships.

Family-of-origin relationships will be based on reality, not on what you would like them to be. Since healthy people are getting their emotional needs met on a regular basis, they do not ask family members to be all things to them. Each family member is seen as an individual, in the present. The decision to risk and be vulnerable with each is based on the safety in that one relationship. Negative feelings from the past have been faced, and there is no need to punish or reject.

You are able to teach others how you wish to be treated, setting limits and expressing feelings as they arise. You are able to reach out and enjoy the good things that exist without resentment about the things that are lacking.

A Strong Identity Is Forming

Strengthening identity is also a process, ever changing through developmental stages. There is, however, a comfort in knowing who you are, a safety in your self-awareness. There are fewer surprises, less vacillating, and less uncertainty. Others cannot consume you, nor can they take away what you know to be true. I-statements are easy to make, since there is a strong *I*.

Among the signs of a strong identity is a certainty about your basic needs, even though your wants may change. It is an ability to hold firm to those needs without trying to adapt and live without them. You have preferences and opinions and express them without fear. Even though you may compromise and negotiate, your beliefs change only when you choose.

You feel connected with your essence, which guides you through your curiosity, inborn abilities, and gifts. You do what gives you joy—music, sports, running, or parenthood—rather than what you feel you are supposed to do. You still have a need for approval, but self-approval is a greater priority. You can risk looking foolish or doing something no one else understands or appreciates.

Your sexual identity has stabilized but continues to grow. You have a stronger sense of your preferences for today but remain open to the possibilities of tomorrow. No other person can define your sexuality. You feel a personal responsibility for your needs and how you express them.

You Are Able to Balance Work and Play

Balance is an elusive goal. You are never fully in it, and you are often fully out of it. As you become healthier, work—the most dangerous area for the perfectionist in the past—changes its focus in your life. Work becomes the means to a quality life, not the life itself. Work is not without joy and reward. Many people are fortunate enough to be able to use their natural gifts and find great satisfaction and fulfillment through work, but it is not as consuming as it once may have been. You may find that although your occupation does not change, your motivation for doing it has become significantly different.

When I first began to work as a therapist, I used my work to survive. It provided distraction from the painful life I was living, and I thrived on the gratitude of those I treated. The greater the intensity of my work, the better I felt. That made working with ACOAs very attractive. Like most compulsive behaviors, my workaholism was not terribly reliable and required more and more stress to maintain the level of intensity I needed. As I grew emotionally, I continued to do similar work, but I no longer needed the intensity. Since I can feel good about myself when I'm doing less, I don't need my work to be the source of all good feelings. Although I may even be more successful today than in the past, I feel much calmer internally. Ironically, the less I need it, the better I perform.

For those who change careers as they grow, work is more carefully chosen, often based on its compatibility with identity, gifts, and lifestyle. Compromises may be made for many good reasons. Some find more joy in an avocation but keep a particular career for financial reward or convenience. The dramatic difference is in the degree of choice and in the absence of a victim or an "I have to do it" way of thinking. The most important thing is that you be true to what you are and that you spend the majority of your time doing something that reflects your essence.

In health, you are learning how to play as well as to balance it with rewarding work. As you let go in one area, you make room for opportunities in another. You are able to play without a goal, an agenda, or a planned outcome.

You Are Willing to Be Vulnerable and Take Risks

Whether involved in a committed relationship, seeking one, or choosing to be alone, healthy people are well enough to be intimate, if they choose. They are not content to live in isolation or superficially with others. They take relationships seriously and do not participate passively when they are in one. Intimacy means more than a sexual connection, and there is a concern both for their own well-being and for that of others.

When you are single, you believe that if and when you choose a partner, you are willing to take the risks involved with getting close. You do not enter close relationships without a consciousness of the effect on yourself and others. There is less fear than before, since you know you have survived before and will be okay.

You worry less about choosing the right person and more about being the right person. It is more important that you concentrate on being truly yourself and having an honest relationship than satisfying the other person in order to keep a mediocre relationship. When you are yourself, honest and open and capable of intimacy, the process of selection is simplified. Those who are healthy are of interest to you; those who are not—*run*!

You Are Ready to Pay It Forward

Full recovery does not mean being self-centered. It is caring about your contribution to making the world a better place. No longer in a perfectionist pattern of looking good and approval seeking, you now have enough of what you need and are ready to be compassionate and generous with balance.

You are ready to accept others as they are while serving as a model of a healthy way of life. Unlike your former perfectionist self, you are approachable and real. Your flaws are showing, and so too is your self-worth. Others find both very attractive and begin to follow without your even noticing.

One day you may wake up and notice that your world has changed. There are no more hurtful people around you, and there is much more humor and joy. People have altered the way they behave toward you. You did nothing directly to make this happen, other than take very good care of yourself. Letting go has made a difference. When you accept people as they are, good things follow.

As a healthy person, you feel a sense of awesome responsibility in being blessed with this opportunity to grow and have a richer, more satisfying life. Gratitude replaces resentment for the painful past that brought you to this point. You observe so many others who are hurting and lost without such opportunities. You feel humbled and free and want very much for others to have the same.

Summary

The signs of health are not a list of "shoulds" to be followed. They are a list of signs that you are moving along in your growth process. Be happy when you notice where you are. This chapter has a couple of tools that I consider essential for managing emotions and peace of mind. One is the meditation, which I do hope you will record and listen to daily or as needed. Another is the suggestion that you develop your own prescription for peace.

There is no destination on this journey, no ending place. You are responsible for how you feel (and it won't always be good), for what you think, and for how you react to what happens around you. If you know yourself well and use all the tools and resources at your disposal, you will find balance—not every day and maybe not all day, but you will hit the target more often than not. There is no coasting in this life. You are moving forward or moving backward. I choose forward most of the time.

The greatest gift we can pay forward is to share our authenticity and vulnerability with the world and especially with the next generation, which, with luck, will not need to work as hard at this as we have. We won't convince them with our words as much as with our beings. Our hope is that they will simply live as healthy individuals who will also make many mistakes and even more improvements over what we were able to provide for them.

The goal, then, is to go full circle—back to where we were headed when we began this journey at birth, enjoying the process and the bumps along the way, being as perfectly imperfect as we can be, and leaving the world a little better than when we entered it.

Acknowledgments

I have so many people to thank for their moral support during the past thirty years of my amazing life and career. My husband is my best friend, my partner in all things, and I'm grateful to him for the boost he gave my career when I started my own business. I wouldn't have been able to develop it without him. To this day, he believes in me and is my best cheerleader.

I could write a book about the greatness of my parents and my sisters, but they wouldn't want me to do that. They have been a constant source of love and support to me and to all of my children. I am proud to be part of such a great, and imperfectly perfect, family.

My children and their children are perfect, in my mind and my heart. I love them for who they are, and I am so grateful that they have embraced our new children and call them family, too. They have all taught me what a healthy family is, even under the most painful and trying circumstances possible.

My friends, most of whom have come from the wonderful staff team at Caron Treatment Centers, are a circle of strong, open, and vulnerable men and women. Marilyn Hawn is the "queen bee" of our "hive." Rosanne Eastman has been a constant source of support, loyalty, and dedication for almost eighteen years, and she is the hub of the wheel of most of what we all do.

I am also grateful to Caron Treatment Centers, the nonprofit addiction treatment center that embraced what I did in 1984 and again in 2009 when they asked me to come back with my five-and-a-half-day Breakthrough Personal Growth Workshops. Caron has given me more opportunities than I can list. I will always have a special place in my heart for the people I have met and learned from on Magic Mountain.

A sincere thanks to Health Communications Inc. and U. S. Journal Training, Inc. for encouraging me to write and speak early in my career, even when I wasn't sure I was ready. Thanks again for bringing me back so that I can share this work with those who need it today.

References

Chapter 1

Rapoport, Judith L. *The Boy Who Couldn't Stop Washing: The Experience and Treatment of Obsessive-Compulsive Disorder*. Markham, ON, Canada: New American Library, 1997.

Chapter 2

Johnson, Susan M., et.al. *Becoming an Emotionally Focused Couples Therapist: The Workbook*. New York: Routledge, Taylor and Francis Group, 2005.

Winnicott, Donald W. "Primary Maternal Preoccupation." *Collected Papers: Through Pediatrics to Psychoanalysis*. London: Tavistock, 1958.

Chapter 3

Smith, Ann W. *Grandchildren of Alcoholics: Another Generation of Co-Dependency*. Deerfield Beach, FL: Health Communications, 1988. (Currently available in e-book through Ann Smith Counseling, e-mail: breakthrough@annsmith.com.)

Chapter 4

Covey, Steven R. *Seven Habits of Highly Effective People: Power Lessons in Personal Change*. New York: Simon and Schuster, 2004.

Chapter 6

Dyer, Wayne W. *The Power of Intention*. Carlsbad, CA: Hay House, 2008.

Williamson, Marianne. *A Return to Love: Reflections on the Principles of a Course in Miracles*. New York: Harper Collins, 1996.

Chapter 8

Johnson, Susan M. *Hold Me Tight: Seven Conversations for a Lifetime of Love*. New York: Little, Brown, 2008.

Chapter 9

Fiore, Neil A. *The Now Habit: A Strategic Program for Overcoming Procrastination and Enjoying Guilt-Free Play*. New York: Penguin, 2007.

Gawain, Shakti, with Laurel King. *Living in the Light: A Guide to Personal and Planetary Transformation.* San Rafael, CA: Whatever Publishing, 1991.

Williamson, Marianne. *Illuminata: Thoughts, Prayers, Rites of Passage*. New York: Random House, 1994.

Recommended Reading

Family Life and Parenting

- *Another Chance: Hope and Health for the Alcoholic Family* by Sharon Wegscheider-Cruse
- *Children: The Challenge: The Classic Work on Improving Parent-Child Relations—Intelligent, Humane & Eminently Practical* by Dr. Rudolph Dreikurs
- *Raising Your Spirited Child: A Guide for Parents Whose Child is More Intense, Sensitive, Perceptive, Persistent, and Energetic* by Mary Sheedy Kurcinka
- *The 7 Habits of Highly Effective Families* by Stephen Covey
- *Step Families: Love, Marriage, and Parenting in the First Decade* by Dr. James H. Bray and John Kelly

Relationships

- *The New Rules of Marriage: What You Need to Know to Make Love Work* by Terrence Real
- *The Dance of Anger: A Woman's Guide to Changing the Patterns of Intimate Relationships* by Harriet Lerner, PhD
- *I Don't Have to Make Everything All Better: Six Practical Principles That Empower Others to Solve Their Own Problems While Enriching Your Relationships* by Gary and Joy Lundberg

- *Hold Me Tight: Seven Conversations for a Lifetime of Love* by Dr. Sue Johnson
- *How Can I Forgive You?: The Courage to Forgive, the Freedom Not To* by Janis Abrahms Spring, PhD
- *The Seven Principles for Making Marriage Work: A Practical Guide from the Country's Foremost Relationship Expert* by John M. Gottman, PhD
- *The Verbally Abusive Relationship: How to Recognize It and How to Respond* by Patricia Evans

Spirituality

- *A New Earth: Awakening to Your Life's Purpose* by Eckhart Tolle
- *A Return to Love: Reflections on the Principles of A Course In Miracles* by Marianne Williamson
- Living in the Light: A Guide to Personal and Planetary Transformation by Shakti Gawain
- The Power of Intention by Wayne W. Dyer
- Illuminata: Thoughts, Prayers, Rites of Passage by Marianne Williamson

About the Author

Ann W. Smith, MS, LMFT, is a nationally recognized leader and expert in the field of relationships and family systems who frequently speaks at major conferences throughout the United States and Canada. A licensed marriage and family therapist, she has spent nearly thirty years helping individuals, couples, and families to achieve a better quality of life.

Ann is the director of Breakthrough at Caron, a residential group program she designed for Caron Treatment Centers that is aimed at helping adults change lifelong patterns, improve relationships, and foster personal growth. This program was featured on NBC's *Dateline* in March 2011.

Ann's professional experience has landed her interviews with National Public Radio, *Newsweek, Us, Redbook, U.S. News & World Report, Philadelphia*, the *Washington Post, Forbes Women*, the *Wall Street Journal*, and numerous other newspapers, magazines, and radio and TV programs across the United States.

Currently, she is a regular contributor to *Psychology Today*'s website through her popular blog, "Healthy Connections," with more than 200,000 views to date. Ann has also authored *Grandchildren of Alcoholics: Another Generation of Co-Dependency*. To learn more about Ann, visit http://www.breakthroughatcaron.org.